Happy Brain,
Happy Life

Maureen H. Cronin

For information, or to order additional copies, contact:

Beacon Publishing Group
P.O. Box 41573 Charleston, S.C., 29423
800.817.8480 / beaconpublishinggroup.com

Publisher's catalog available upon request.

ISBN-13: 978-1-949472-09-7

ISBN-10: 1-949472-09-7

Published in 2020. New York, NY 10001.

First Edition

Printed in the USA

Table of Contents

1

The Happiness Concept

Are you happy?

Who *is* happy? Not just having a good day happy. But truly deeply happy from inside. Happiness that is not dependent on having a loving partner, or oodles of money in the bank, or a loving family, or a big home, or the car of your dreams.

Happiness. It's an overused word and no one really knows what it means. *Are you happy?*, you ask your friend or sister or brother when they get married. As long as you're happy, you say. Knowing there will be days where they are decidedly *not* happy, when the rote-ness of the marriage feels lackluster. The baby you once cuddled, as you felt your love overwhelm you, is now a sullen middle schooler, or a snotty teenager that wants nothing to do with you. Within that sullenness or snottiness or ennui, however, there are small moments, moments where you know the love is there, waiting and watching for a small crumb that falls to the floor, eagerly snapping it up as if there will never be another.

So with all the realities of life – money, marriage, children, love, loneliness, stress, boredom – how *can* we be truly happy?

I'll tell you. It's not easy. Happiness is a simple concept, but one of the hardest to truly achieve. I read *The Road Less Traveled* by M. Scott Peck years ago, and one of the first lines (I'm paraphrasing) is "Life is difficult. Once you accept the difficulty, your transcend it."

Let's look at the word *transcend*. It means to "be or go beyond the range or limits of something abstract." *Go beyond the limits of something abstract.* What the hell? Yeah. It took me awhile too. Here's how I did it.

I started writing this in my early forties, but I was not healed yet. I had no happy ending. I have never been married. I do not have any children of my own. I tried to have children for a long time. I went through years of IVF cycles. I gained an enormous amount of weight from the medications and subsequent depression. I got pregnant a few times and miscarried. I had an ectopic that took my fallopian tube and the other tube was damaged. Or toxic. Or unexplained infertility disorder. *Whatever*.

Those of you who have been through this, I don't have to tell you about the heart-wrenching sorrow of yet another failure. The one person who said to me, "that which does not break you, makes you stronger", I didn't speak to for five years.

I tried adopting after that. That too was expensive. I spent thousands on advertising and a website. I fielded calls from liars and demented people that wanted to know what color my nipples were. I got taken for a few thousand dollars by a drug addicted woman in New Hampshire who gave birth to a cocaine-addicted baby and said she never planned to let me adopt the baby anyway. She just wanted the money. She disappeared under the radar after that. On this same day,

I managed to get my cheating, narcissistic boyfriend out of my home for good.

It was a sad movie that played over and over again for all those years. I was angry. I was afraid that I would become bitter. Why me? What the EFF God?

I had prayed and prayed and prayed. I wanted an explanation. I wanted answers. I wanted guarantees. Did God really not want me to be a mother? Did God not want me to prosper?

No. That is not true. We are responsible for all the decisions we make in our lives. I decided to use my money for IVF, year after year, watching my friends have babies and brag about their smallest accomplishments on social media. I allowed myself to be party to bad, unloving relationships.

For years after, anytime I met someone new, they would invariably ask: Are you married? Do you have kids? It was like a knife going through me. Smiling and swallowing the pain behind the answer.

It sucked. I was living in a private hell of pretending. I wanted to heal. I wanted to be happy. I knew I needed a spiritual makeover.

And this is where my happiness began: down in the fifth ring of hell of my inner self.

2

Enough is Enough

Anger is a tough one. Justified anger is even worse. What jury in the world would convict me of being angry and bitter because I was childless after all I had been through? All the tears and disappointments. I wore sadness like a protective coating, preventing anyone from getting too close to me. I dated men I would not fall in love with, nor would I grow to love, because I couldn't stand the pain of loving and losing.

Finally, I had had enough. I started doing things I loved. Painting, writing, singing, telling my close friends and family how much I loved them. Heartfelt conversations that were filled with laughter and tears and years of knowing each other.

A friend took me for a Reiki healing. Turns out my left ovary was toxic. Or so this Reiki Master said. She showed me the shiny pink quartz crystal before she placed it on my body. She showed it to me after it had lain there for a few minutes. The shiny pink finish was gray. Terrific. Where was she three years ago when I started IVF? Yet I still knew women with busted up insides that were able to conceive, so I was still angry about it.

The answer lay in acceptance. Once I accepted it, I did transcend the difficulty.

But I still needed to work on the anger.

I started focusing on the things in my life that were purely good. My relationship with my mother. My siblings. Their children. I love my nieces and my nephew. I see three of my nieces regularly. We have play dates and sleepovers and we paint and bake together. The youngest one still runs and jumps into my arms every time she sees me. There is nothing in the world better than that feeling.

I began to see how I was positively influencing their lives. How they are all brilliant in their own ways. How talented they all are - and how confident they are about that talent, their artwork. I see how they love me – unconditionally – and I make sure to tell them I love them unconditionally. Had I had children of my own as a single woman, would I have been able to affect this level of influence over them? No. I would not have had the time or the energy. I don't know how I will influence their lives as they grow into young men and women and adults. I don't know what memories they will hold forever in their hearts. But I know that I have plenty of them. My brain wanted more of this good feeling – a feeling I later identified as dopamine.

The brain is a funny thing. A certain smell can send me into a memory so deeply it feels as if I am there. A song does that too.

Then I knew. It's the brain that heals the heart.

It takes training and retraining. It takes practice. We need to actively practice happiness so that we retrain our brains for positivity. Remember that I first had to practice acceptance. Once the acceptance took hold, it opened the pathway for me to let go. Mind you, I still took my will and my pain back on occasion, but I continued to practice happiness until I was finally accepting of my life. It was only then that the inner happiness truly began to surface.

3

The Healing Brain

I call it the healing brain. Some might call it survival instinct, but it's more than that. Survival instinct is a behavior that is mediated by reactions below the conscious level. Fight or flight. It was my first reaction to all the disappointment. First I fought, then I flew away. The survival instinct does not heal; it protects.

I started reading about healing modalities and methods. I decided to study Reiki. I cleared out my second bedroom. I gave the bassinet, changing table, diaper bags, and the little baby socks I had obsessively collected over the years to a friend who had had a successful IVF at the age of 40. I gave the crib to the Salvation Army. I bought a bed for that room. I read up on the power of aromatherapy and crystals. I read about healing in all walks of life. I read about honest-to-God miracles. I tried meditation. Some of you may think I went over the top –

you're entitled to that opinion. But I am here to tell you that it was my brain and not my heart that led me to this.

I started to feel an inner shift. This did not happen overnight. As I slowly focused on happiness and reminded myself to focus on happiness when the sadness or frustration hit me, it started to work. *I had to practice the happiness*, remind myself to keep my focus there. It's like a diet. You start a diet. You're focused. You lose 10 pounds. You start to lose your focus looking at the second piece of cake or another roll at dinner. You are faced with a decision: do you want to feel good about your body, or do you want to feel temporary happiness and subsequent depression?

We are in charge of how we feel. Our brains can be retrained. This is a belief system that will work. We have to shut down the impulse meter and literally move our thoughts to the long-term positive.

That's what I practiced. Eventually it became a way of life.

4

Intuition v. Logic

Unfortunately, we live in a world that worships logic over intuition. Who can argue with $1 + 1 = 2$? That's logic. But 1+1 can equal three – if the 1+1 make a baby. That's intuitive. Why is Google so successful? Because they married logic and intuition. They took their logic, and they matched it with the intuitive thought of "how will people search for this?" And wham. They're ready to challenge the Klingons for interstellar domination at this point.

I lead with the heart almost all the time. Like most qualities, it's a double-edged sword. But my brain started to take over because my heart recognized the healing impact it was having.

The brain is designed to adapt. Continually. Exercising it is the key. Just as we exercise our bodies, and yoga teaches us to breathe to exercise our inner organs, the brain needs that type of stimulation too.

My first proof of using my own brain to heal me was a long time ago. I was in college and my parents were going through a horrific divorce. I began having a recurring nightmare over and over. I would wake in a cold sweat and filled with fear. It was hard for me to go back to sleep. I would think while I was in the dream, "*Oh no, not this dream again.*"

I realized I was talking to myself in the dream. That my logical, waking brain was functioning within this nightmare, and that if that was happening, maybe I could tell my brain to change it.

It was worth a try. I wanted more awareness of the dream state, so I started keeping a journal of whatever I could remember from any dream as soon as I woke up. The color red, for example. A person. A balloon in the sky. This was a practice. After about a week, I was remembering more and more of my dreams. When the nightmare came again, I said, *I am changing this. I am able to fly away from this scary situation and never go back. I am turning this scary monster into an insect that flies away. I am able to watch you disintegrate before my eyes. This is my dream and I control it.*

It worked. Then I decided I wanted to do more than just fly away. I wanted to confront the fear. The next time I had any inkling of a scary dream, I turned to face whatever monster had manifested as my fear and I said, *"This is my dream"* and screamed at it: *"You can't scare me so go away!"* I then made said monster turn and walk away and disappear.

My brain was now working with me. That was my first proof that the brain can adapt and heal.

I've read all about the power of affirmations and living a grateful life. But for me, I had to back into acceptance first, let that settle in and the figure out the healing part. Knowing that I had changed my brain to reprogram a disturbing dream made me think that I could take it further. I started researching. It's one thing to believe in yourself; that takes practice and it is not always easy. When I found scientific research to support the fact that the brain actually changes, I was off to the races.

5

It's All In Your Head

After years of trying to become a mother every which way, and spending *alllllll* my money, I studied Reiki enough to become a Reiki Master. I studied the chakras of the body and how they represent core areas of our belief systems. I used chakra meditations to turn off my brain and to help me get to sleep at night. I did a heart wall removal and soul retrieval which I will speak more about later. I found like-minded people. I read Deepak Chopra and his journey to this mindfulness. I read Goldie Hawn's book (yes *that* Goldie Hawn) on the benefits of mindfulness meditation. She started a foundation called MindUp to help children deal with grief and stress. I recommend it to everyone of all ages.

I read studies conducted by neuroscientists with degrees from Harvard and MIT.

You know that old saying, *"It's all in your head"*?

It is.

Our brains are amazing. They are working all the time in a million different directions at warp speed. We are constantly taking in information, processing it, categorizing it, and acting on it all within milliseconds. There's left brain and right brain functions. They are literally split in half so they are equal in size and importance. The right brain controls creativity, imagination, intuition, holistic thought, music awareness, and left-hand movement. The left brain controls analytical thought, logic, language, science, math, written abilities, number skills, and right-hand movement. An easy way to remember this is that left-handed people are the only ones in their "right" minds, because the right side of the brain directs left-hand controls. (Guess which one I am?)

A few more scientific facts. The medulla oblongata controls brain stem or life-sustaining functions like breathing, swallowing, and heart rate. I remember it by thinking of an obLONGata stem, like the long stem giving nutrients to the flower.

The cerebellum is in charge of balance, coordination and muscle functions. The word sounds like a kind of dance for me – everyone do the cerebellum – so it helps me remember it is about balance and coordination which we need to dance. The hypothalamus controls hunger, thirst, and body temperature. HHH: H for hypothalamus, H for hunger, H for hot.

The amygdala is where we hold anxiety, fear, and stress. Think of it like an ambulance rushing to the scene. A for amygdala, A for ambulance.

The hippocampus handles long term memory and emotional responses. Strangely enough, this part of the brain is very small, incongruous to the hippo part of the name, so it's like someone big and tall named Tiny.

The thalamus relays information from the sensory receptors and processes it: auditory, tactile, and taste. Essentially the thalamus talks to the body, and I imagine its speaking voice in a lisp. That helps me remember the thalamus name.

Those are the basics.

For purposes of this book, I am going to focus on the hippocampus and the amygdala. You'll soon see why.

6 Proof Positive

In my initial research, I found Masuro Emoto's study of water. He was a doctor of Alternative Medicine in Japan. His book, *The Hidden Message of Water*, was a *New York Times* bestseller. He claimed that human consciousness has an effect on the molecular structure of water. He believed that water could react to positive thoughts and words, and that polluted water could be cleaned through prayer and positive visualization. Loosely explained, Emoto's study involved two test groups of water. One group was told to speak lovingly to one jar of water; the other was told to harshly criticize the other jar. This tenet was based on the fact that we are water. As fetuses we are 99% water; as adults we are 70% percent water. Therefore, we exist mostly as water.

Within the study's timetable, there were subtle differences in the microscopic molecules of each jar of water. The water that was given positive messages or prayer was clearer and shinier. The jar that was given negative messages was not as clear or shiny. And while there is criticism for some of his findings, it made sense to me. So if we, as predominantly water, believe ourselves to be wrong somehow, or depressed, or negative, or 'woe is me', or worse, we tell ourselves we are not lovable because we are too much or not enough, that is what the brain reacts to. We then become that. If negativity can have *any* effect on water, what is it doing to us?

Then I found Sara Lazar, PhD, a neuroscientist at Harvard, who published an article the benefits of meditation and mindfulness in the *Washington Post* in May of 2015, citing scientific evidence that is undisputed.

The hippocampus is the part of the brain that controls memory and learning. The amygdala (pronounced: eh-mig-dill-a) is a brain region associated with anxiety and stress. Both of these areas house gray matter. Lazar's 2011 study discovered that people who meditated 30 minutes a day for eight weeks had increased gray matter in the hippocampus (memory and learning), and a reduction of gray matter in the amygdala (anxiety and stress). There were no changes in the brain matter of the control group that didn't perform mindfulness meditation.

What does that tell us? That meditation is proven to improve memory and learning while reducing stress and anxiety. There's more though. If you've suffered a trauma, and you repress that trauma, your brain is holding that trauma in the stress and anxiety area. To put it in laymen's terms, it's akin to that area of the brain growing, leaving less room for new memory and new learning. That cycle affects your actions, decisions, and behaviors. If our actions, decisions, and behaviors are stemming from the anxiety and stress core of our brains, then we are motivated from that point. And if we are motivated from that point, we are making decisions rooted in fear, stress, and anxiety. That then creates a cycle of anxiety or worse in our lives.

Dr. Oz did a show on this as well. He looked at the brain of a deceased monk who meditated daily for his entire life and compared it to the brain of someone the same age who did not meditate. The hippocampus (memory and learning) was noticeably larger in the monk's brain. The amygdala (anxiety and stress) was noticeably smaller.

Women – as a general rule – have better connections to the amygdala – which is like an alarm in the body. It's the part that makes us react quickly, or too quickly, or say things in anger. When we get upset and we are holding anger or stress, the amygdala starts firing. How many of us women have been accused of being too emotional – especially in conflict with a man? Blame the amygdala. If we can learn to calm ourselves down first by breathing deeply before we react, the amygdala calms down and the prefrontal lobe lights up. The prefrontal lobe is like our inner control panel. It monitors emotional expression, problem solving, memory, language, judgment, sexual behavior, communication. You want to be coming from that prefrontal lobe area in an emotional conflict.

Neuroscientists have studied brain reactions to varying stimuli. Different mental activities actually change brainwave patterns. For example, a musician may have areas of the brain that are thicker in relation to fine motor skills.

As your brain changes, you experience changes. Caffeine stimulates; alcohol relaxes.

Consider these findings from a study by Dr. Rick Hanson:

- Activating the left frontal regions leads to a sunnier outlook and more positive mood – while strokes in those areas leave patients particularly irritable and depressed.

- The brains of mediators are thicker in the regions engaged with sensory awareness and with the control of attention.

- The brains of taxi drivers are thicker in the regions that are key to visual-spatial memories.

- Surges of the neurotransmitter dopamine feel very pleasurable. This is why dopamine is associated with addictions.

Let's look at how joy manifests in the body. The positive benefits of happy, joyful experiences can literally reduce stress in our bodies by dampening the arousal of the sympathetic nervous system ("fight or flight") and by activating the parasympathetic nervous system (relaxed and contented). Positive feelings reduce the impact of stress on our cardiovascular systems. They increase psychological resilience, lift moods, protect against depression, and promote optimism. Over time, they help counteract the effects of trauma or other painful experiences. When you remember something painful from your past, your brain first reconstructs that memory – including its emotional associations – and reconstitutes it in storage *with remnants of your state of mind at the time you recalled it*. This means that if you were feeling sad or negative or angry in the time of the actual memory, then your recollection of it will be increasingly negative. Alternately, if you recall it repeatedly with a realistically upbeat state of being, then it will gradually come to mind more and more with a more neutral quality: you will not forget the facts of what happened, but their emotional impact will slowly fade – and that can be a great relief.

This results in highlighted key states of mind so you can find your way back to them in the future – and can more readily tap into peace, contentment, strength, well-being, etc. It's like getting a reward for doing something that's noble but not always easy, thus supporting ongoing motivation. All these benefits also work for children, by the way.

Even minor or fleeting experiences leave traces in the brain. Consider your dream state. How often has someone you know well had a different face in the dream, yet you *know* it's them in the dream? The face could be someone you passed on the street or saw in a restaurant – yesterday or five years ago. Our thoughts are in a constant state of stream of consciousness that leave marks on our brains. How this information is assimilated and manifested can depend on your state of mind.

Say we both dream about apples. If I used to pick apples with my very kind grandfather, apples have a positive connotation. But if I was pelted with apples in kindergarten by mean-spirited classmates, apples would symbolize negativity and betrayal in my brain and manifest as such.

Your experiences are important not just because of their brief effects on your subjective quality of life, but also because they produce enduring changes in the physical structures of your brain. And these affect your well-being, functioning, and sometimes your physical health for days and decades to come. This affects you and others because your reasoning is subjective to your brain training.

So what do we know now? We know that we are tied to our memories, and that memories associated with fear and anxiety take precedence in our brains. We act based on these tightly-held beliefs and that can prevent us from fully enjoying our lives or experiencing true happiness.

Practicing brain balance is important. Making sure we increase our positive memory databank is even more important, as you will see in the coming chapters.

7

Like The Corners Of Your Mind

There are two kinds of memory: explicit and implicit. Explicit memory can recall specific events in detail. Implicit memory is emotion-based: body sensations, relationship paradigms, your view of the world. Implicit memories are your "gut" feelings. They are visceral memories that slowly build your living experience. It's what we mix into ourselves; just as food is mixed into our bodies, implicit memories become woven into ourselves.

Unfortunately, the brain remembers and focuses on negative experiences. This is not all bad because recalling negative experience is how we learn life lessons sometimes. How many times do you grab a hot pot before you learn not to?

This negative focus actually stems from our ancestors because our ancestral memories are part of the DNA in our brains. According to a study by neuroscientist Mike McConnell of the University of Virginia, "every neuron probably has a unique genome. That variation may have important implications for how the brain grows and functions normally, and for when problems arise. We're no longer saying, 'Do neurons have different genomes? We're saying, let's figure out how that matters." [1]

In a nutshell, it's how we know things we never learned.

In 1940, A.A. Brill quoted Dr. William Carpenter who, while comparing math prodigy Zerah Colburn's calculating powers to Mozart's mastery of musical composition, supports this ancestral knowledge:
"In each of the foregoing cases, then, we have a peculiar example of the possession of an extraordinary congenital aptitude for certain mental activity, which showed itself at so early a period as to exclude the notion that it could have been acquired by the experience of the individual. To such

congenital gifts we give the name of intuitions: it can scarcely be questioned that like the instincts of the lower animals, they are the expressions of constitutional tendencies embodied in the organism of the individuals who manifest them."

Okay. That's a mouthful. The point is, we all know this is true. We have seen it. We have witnessed it. We have experienced it. There are studies that prove it.

Can we train ourselves to listen to our "gut" instincts? Can we increase positive memories in our brains?

Yes. There is a primal source in all of us. And you will soon learn that we have ancestral data and even predisposed emotional conditions that are inherited. This cannot be dismissed if we are to practice and live truly happy lives.

8

The Lizard Brain

Consider the primal aspects of the "Lizard Brain" – our fight or flight instincts. We all have it. Animals have it in spades. Try sneaking up on a sleeping dog. They will either turn to you, their ears will move, or they will rise – all indicating the awareness of your presence. They then determine whether this is a safe situation or a fearful one. If fearful, the brain measures the fear for the flight or fight reaction.

The limbic system of the brain monitors other primal urges such as emotional bonding to animals or people, hunger, fear, and sexual needs.

If we look at evolution as an example, smaller animals learned to be aware of larger, more dangerous creatures such as dinosaurs. They learned – their brains learned – to be alert to the slightest change in the environment – like a twig snapping or bushes rustling – and their lizard brains determine the level of danger to their survival and they reacted accordingly.

Consider the phrase: the calm before the storm. When warm, moist air is pulled into a storm system, it leaves a low pressure vacuum in its wake. The air travels up through the storm cloud and helps fuel it. The updrafts in the storm, however, carry the air upward, and when it reaches the top of the cloud mass, this warm moist air gets spit out at the top. The air is sent rolling out over the big, anvil-shaped head of the thunderclouds or the rolling arms of hurricanes. From there, the air descends – drawn back toward lower altitudes by the very vacuum its departure created in the first place.

Over the years, people dependent on the environment for their survival – farmers for instance – had to teach their brains to recognize the patterns of weather and what it meant; animals even more so. When that vacuum occurs, we'll see birds flying in the

sky, horses going back into their stalls,
insects finding shelter. Their lizard brains are
protecting them.

That same circuitry is wired in our brains as
we drive through traffic, argue with a mate,
or hear an odd noise in the night. First, the
amygdala (our anxiety and stress
switchboard) directs a response (approach,
avoid, move on) – because it is
neurologically programmed to label
experiences as frightening and negative. In
other words, it's built to *look* for the bad. For
example, when someone gives you feedback
– a parent, friend, lover, or boss – does your
mind sometimes go looking for the hint of
criticism surrounded by praise?

Second, when an event is flagged as
negative, the amygdala-hippocampus
partnership immediately stores it for future
reference. Then it compares current events
to the archive of painful ones, and if there
are any similarities, your alarms start going
off. Once burned, twice shy. Your brain
doesn't just go looking for what's negative;

it's built to grab that information and hold on for dear life.

Yes, we can notice positive experiences and remember them. But unless what you're remembering is a one-in-a-million moment, the brain circuitry for what is positive is like writing something down compared to a monster computer with terabyte storage for what is negative.

If you go over your day at night, do you see the dozens of nice and pleasant moments, or the awkward, frustrating, or challenging moments? When you look back on your life, what do you see: the millions of pleasures and accomplishments, or the handful of losses and failures?

The negative generally trumps the positive: A single bad event for a dog is more memorable than 100 good ones. A study by Martin Seligman and his colleagues show that it took only a short time to induce a sense of helplessness in the dogs, whose brain circuitry for emotional memory is very similar to our own. But it took an extraordinary effort to get them to unlearn that training. It's as if we are predisposed to believe the worst about the world and ourselves, and to doubt the best.

My mother never liked dogs. She was attacked and bitten by a dog at an early age. We finally convinced her to get a dog. A friend of the family, who was a military man, (I'll explain why this detail is necessary in a minute) bred Labradors. We got Dewey at eight weeks. A gentle, beautiful Golden Lab. He barked ferociously at the mailman. Every. Single. Day. But that's what dogs do right? They protect their castle. One day, five years later, my father, who bonded with Dewey right away, and frankly, provided most of the training, walked into the house wearing his old army jacket. Dewey backed away, hackles up, teeth gnashing, growling at my father. My father kept saying "Dewey, it's me, listen to my voice, it's okay boy."

It wasn't until my father removed his army jacket that Dewey calmed down, went to him tail down and licked his hand. We found out years later, that Dewey had been kicked by one of the military men in the house – somewhere in his first 8 weeks of life. His lizard brain captured this one event early in his life, and the five years of love and attention did nothing to make it go away.

My mother's opinion of dogs was reinforced by that incident, and she remained distant from Dewey ever after.

Your own personal training in the negative – whatever it's been – shapes your view of the world and yourself, and your personality and interpersonal style and approach to life. In the extreme, such as with a serious history of trauma or depression, the hippocampus can actually shrink up to 20%, impairing the brain's capacity to even *remember* positive experiences.

All that can lead to more of the negative showing up on your radar – which, in a vicious cycle, can make you even more inclined to see and even *cause* the negative in the future – despite the fact that the actual data of the majority of said events and experiences in your life are neutral or positive. Every day, our minds render verdicts about our character, our life, and our future possibilities that are profoundly unfair.

This is why practicing happiness is so important to balance out our brains, and subsequently, our behaviors.

And, it bears repeating, one of the best ways to practice happiness daily is to practice meditation.

9

The Mystery Of Life

But how? Who has time to actually meditate? Let's first look at the definition of the word meditate: *to think deeply or focus one's mind for a period of time as a method of relaxation; to think deeply or carefully about (something); to plan mentally or consider.*

That's it. Chanting is optional. Music is optional. If you mentally focus on one thing, like happiness, you will feel happy. Conversely, if you focus on something negative, like "I'm going to freeze during my presentation to the boss today" or "this is going to be a bad day", you will feel negative and therefore suppress anything positive energy that might happen in the course of the day. You might even manifest messing up in your presentation. Our energy flows where our attention goes.

It's important to note here that we can also only change the way *we* feel about a person or situation. We can very rarely change another person unless they are open to the change. As individuals, we *can* help emphasize and store positive experiences through conscious attention.

Remember the adage "Be careful what you wish for?" Mental meditation, positive or negative, can actually create the outcome you fear or the situation you want. The key is understanding that we have no control over the outcome or over other people. We need to let go of the outcome and do the best we can. That's it.

I got laid off from a job I loved. I was angry and frustrated. I was embarrassed. I missed my work friends. I missed the paycheck. I was constantly checking my account balance. I spent my free mornings submitting resume after resume for everything I could find. My frustration grew as my weeks of unemployment dragged on. At some point I realized that I might as well make the best of my unemployment. I started hitting the gym at off hours in the morning when it was not crowded. I spent time with friends who were home during the day. I took some road trips to see family in nearby states.

I made sure to spend the first hour or two of the day looking for jobs that I wanted and that I was qualified for – not overqualified or underqualified – but appropriate to my experience. I was more focused. I let go of the outcome knowing I had done the best I could for that day.

I did get a job within 8 weeks of being laid off, and looking back, it is a blip on the radar of my life. The first few weeks were filled with mental panic, some denial, anger, and the why me's. Once I accepted my circumstances – I'm unemployed, now what? – I had to relax my brain, exercise, refocus my goal, and let go of the outcome.

Anything we focus on intently can be a form of meditation. I'm a swimmer, and I use headphones that work underwater. Once I put those headphones on and my music starts to play, and I start to swim, I am in a different place. Some of you may have experienced this yourselves. Even if I don't swim hard that particular day, or beat my previous times, I always enjoy a trifecta of mind-body-soul relaxation afterwards.

Back to the positively focused brain. As we know from school, we remember something best when we make it as vivid as possible and then give it heightened attention over an extended period. That's exactly how to register positive experiences in your implicit memory – which will slowly but surely change the interior landscape of your mind.

Similarly, we can relive good, exciting, or positive experiences by simply letting them replay in our minds. We can talk with other people about said positive experiences. We can pay close attention to the good things about ourselves and our lives. We can decide to write down 1-5 things we are currently grateful for every morning or every night. Or simply recite those grateful things in our minds in the morning. We can actively look for beauty in our world, our good qualities, and how people that care about us express that. We can decide not to be around people that are negative or make us feel anxious or sad.

This is not to negate mourning periods during times of loss. When my father died suddenly from an aneurysm, the sadness was ineffable. I cried every day on my way to work for weeks. I could barely accept any offering of condolence from outside my family. I could vividly see how he looked in the hospital that last day, my siblings crying, inconsolable, as I was.

Yet I knew, intellectually, that my father would not want me to go around crying every morning. Eventually I allowed myself to let the sadness come, but I started to allow it to leave as well. I want to repeat that. *I allowed it to leave.*

This is also a survival instinct. It's *emotional survival.* I could not stay in that all-consuming sadness for any length of time and continue to be a functioning person. I needed a distraction. I bought CDs to learn French to occupy my brain during the drive to work and back. I downloaded happy songs that made me smile.

It took a while. It took practice. The loss of a loved one leaves scar tissue in a big way. But we heal. We do heal.

Slowly but surely, I centered my thoughts of my father around all the funny things he did and said and the great moments we had between us. My siblings and I talk about him often. We'll often tell each other, "That's so Daddy" when one of us does something just the way Dad would have. I focus on those memories and use them like a sunny blanket around the loss.

We do not forget, but it balances out the sadness. And that's what I'm talking about.

10

Fiddle Dee Dee

Many people who have experienced emotional trauma subscribe to what I call the Scarlett O'Hara school of thought: *Fiddle dee dee. I won't think about that now, I'll think about it tomorrow.*

I'm here to tell you that any trauma you bury will come back biting in one form or another. Traumas, from severe, ongoing childhood abuse to divorce or death, hide like dark rivers in the brain. The more severe the trauma, the deeper the river.

While repression can be a primal self-defense mechanism, eventually the repressed memory or memories will surface. When they do surface, it's anyone's guess as to how. A person could develop anything from depression to a split personality or other more severe dissociative disorders.

Northwestern Medicine released their findings on this in August of 2015. There are several pathways for the brain to store fear-inducing memories. But repression can be so severe that one of the only ways to access these memories is to relax the brain to the point where they can surface.

Principal investigator Dr. Jelena Radulovic, the Dunbar Professor in Bipolar Disease at Northwestern University Feinberg School of Medicine, explains brain functions like an AM/FM radio station. "The brain functions in different states, much like a radio operates at AM and FM frequency bands," Radulovic said. "It's as if the brain is normally tuned to FM stations to access memories but needs to be tuned to AM stations to access subconscious memories. If a traumatic event occurs when these extra-synaptic GABA receptors are activated, the memory of this event cannot be accessed unless these receptors are activated once again, essentially tuning the brain into the AM stations."

That's one of the better explanations I found for this phenomenon. Essentially, traumas need to be uncovered and remembered if we are to heal the brain.

For those of us who *are* aware of our traumas, we still may not realize how said trauma has assimilated into our makeup and how it drives our behaviors, social aptitudes, and outlook on life.

Therefore, maintaining a positive state of mind is much more than a platitude. We need to actively balance our brain by acknowledging trauma – and letting it go.

So there's the science. I did not know all this before I started meditating and practicing joy. All I knew is that being unhappy was no way to go through life.

11
The Yellow Brick Road

Decide to let yourself feel pleasure and be happy, rather than feel guilty about enjoying life. Decide to be quietly inclined to joy. Let there be no limits to how good you can feel about yourself and your life. Just decide that.

This will open up the sensate aspects of your responses to positive events, and that is your first step on the yellow brick road. It's like deciding to live your life in full color.

Do things that make you happy. Find people in your life that make you happy. Bring to mind the feelings of love and compassion, recall the memories and senses of feeling purely content, peaceful, and happy.

Think of one of those memories now. Smile. (Smiling also has a physiological response in the brain – even a forced smile.) Remember everything you can about this memory.

Extend this event in time and space. Linger in this memory. Keep your attention focused on this very pleasant, peaceful, joyful moment. If you feel a little uncomfortable, stay with it anyway. Think about the person you were with or the smells around you. If you were touched, remember the touch.

Imagine this peace and contentment filling your body like a warm light. Send it throughout your body and imagine it in your heart, expanding your heart, down through your torso, your legs, your arms, your toes and fingers. *Feel* how this feels. Smile. Close your eyes. Love this moment in time.

Breathe in and out deeply and completely.

Open your eyes.

Guess what? You just meditated. Even if you kept your eyes open.

Try it. Set a timer to 60 seconds and repeat the above meditation for three days in a row. I was amazed at the results. The first day I looked at my timer twice: at 20 seconds and 40 seconds, but I just went back into the memory and relived it over and over. By the third day, I could not believe how quickly the 60 seconds had passed.

This practice essentially opens up the floodgates of positive experience in your brain, releasing dopamine, which is our feel-good part of the brain. You are simultaneously crowding out negative emotions and replacing them with this feel-good moment.

Doesn't it feel good? Don't *you* feel good?

We're all broken in some way. We've all gone through losses and sadness and traumas. Practicing happiness through meditation is how I fill those cracks. There's a Japanese philosophy called *kintsugi*. It's the art of repairing broken pottery with lacquer mixed with powdered gold, silver, or platinum. The broken piece becomes even more valuable and beautiful as its cracks are filled with gold, making the brokenness part of the object's history, rather than something to disguise or discard.

This philosophy embraces the brokenness and adds value to the object *because of* that brokenness. That's what we need to do with ourselves. This is not about hiding or disguising our own brokenness but celebrating it as part of the whole of us and filling ourselves and others up with pieces of liquid gold that shimmer and shine throughout our lives.

12

The Balance of Power

By focusing on positive stimuli, which tends to roll through us quickly, we help them sink in. This balances out and even overrides the negative stimuli that automatically get captured and deferred to.

Now that you know all that, why would you not want to practice happiness?

Meditation for me was the best way to get to the happy place. It's not as hard as you think. I did not pick it up right away. But I did not dismiss it because I wasn't "good" at it. I put quotes around the word "good" because that was my own definition, my own negative brain dismissing it. I found two-minute meditations I liked and downloaded them to my phone. I started listening to them in the car on my commute to work. I recognize this as multi-tasking, and probably not what the Buddhists Monks have in mind, but it started to work for me. I did not close my eyes obviously, but I did feel a sense of comfort in the private cocoon of my car. It felt nice. It felt like I was taking action in my life to be more positive. I graduated to 15- and 20-minute meditations and began using longer meditations at night, which was the best time of day for me to relax. I *practiced* it. I began to cultivate it as a habit. I began to see what all the fuss was about.

Back to my starting point. I started with one minute of deep breathing. I focused on a pleasant image, like the sun setting on the ocean. I imagined feeling the warmth of the sun on my skin, the cool breeze from the ocean, the sand in my toes. I did the deep in-through-the-nose-out-through-the-mouth breathing. I smiled. I relaxed my shoulders. Sometimes I rolled them back a bit. I let my chin drop to my chest and rolled it slowly to the right shoulder and around to the left. I felt my body relaxing. After a few days of this practice, I felt my mind relaxing. I began to have more focus and clarity.

One of the things I teach in my writing classes is how to relax the brain. Have you ever lost something? And then gone crazy looking for it? Of course you have. What happens if you can't find it? You give up. You do something else. The next morning in the shower, or on your way to work, or in the middle of your exercise, you suddenly remember where you left the thing you lost. Why does this happen? Because you have relaxed the brain enough for it to access that memory. If you are struggling with something like a lost item, or a solution to a problem at work, or writer's block, you are essentially flooding your brain – the amygdala – with stress and alarm bells. It's like strangling the brain. The best thing you can do is stop thinking about it. This allows the amygdala to calm down, and subsequently allows the hippocampus to take the driver's seat.

Back to meditation. As I continued my meditation practice, I gave myself permission to not be perfect. I allowed myself to practice it in a way that made me feel comfortable and accomplished. I increased my practice to two minutes. I added music sometimes. I found myself smiling throughout it. I visualized scenarios in my life that I wanted to manifest.

Here's what started to change: Increased self-esteem. General happiness. Physical fitness. Healthy eating. Telling people how important they are to me. Random acts of kindness. Doing the next right thing even when it was the harder thing (which is usually the case). My artwork improved. My patience levels increased. I was more focused at work. I felt happier. I *was* happier. People were genuinely happy to see me – even strangers on the street smiled more at me.

Happiness takes practice. Sometimes it's work. There are moments in life when it just happens to us –those moments I hope we all get loads of – but we need to do the work to remember them, dwell on them, and give our positive brains a fighting chance.

13

Mind Your Mindfulness

Meditation has long been associated with decreased stress, depression, anxiety, pain, and insomnia, and an increased quality of life.

In a recent study, people who had never meditated before were put through an eight-week mindfulness stress reduction program.

A study of long-term meditators and a control group found that the meditators had an increased amount of gray matter in the insula and sensory regions, the auditory and sensory cortex. This makes sense, because when you're mindful, you're paying attention to your breathing, to sounds, to the present moment experience, while shutting cognition down. It stands to reason your senses would be enhanced.

Long-term meditators also had more gray matter in the frontal cortex, which is associated with working memory and executive decision-making. Our cortex shrinks as we get older – it's harder to figure things out and remember things. But in this one region of the prefrontal cortex, 50-year-old meditators had the same amount of gray matter as 25-year-olds.

Think of meditation as an everyday task, like brushing your teeth. Make it a habit and get your brain and body used to the downtime. Try doing it in your car on your way to work, or just if you find yourself alone in the car for a period of time. Do whatever it takes to establish a routine. Find a private spot in your home. You can sit in a certain position, but you don't have to. You do not need to sit cross-legged or chant. The point is to be comfortable as this will help the process. Chanting helps quiet your brain because it forces the brain to focus on it. Sometimes I just monitor my breath and say to myself: I am breathing in; I am breathing out. That keeps my brain engaged enough to stop the background chatter. The whole point of mindfulness meditation is to anchor your mind in the present and not allow it time to travel to the past and the future, which it does at lightning speed almost 24/7.

Again: it takes practice. And while perfection may be your direction, it is not the goal. A recent study conducted by The Hawn Foundation (MindUp) found differences in brain volume after eight weeks in five different regions in the brains of the two groups. In the group that learned meditation, there was thickening in four regions:

1. The posterior cingulate, which is mind wandering, and self-relevance – thereby increasing focus.

2. The left hippocampus, which assists in learning, cognition, memory and emotional regulation and increasing the capacity for new, pleasant memories.

3. The temporo parietal junction, or TPJ, which is associated with perspective taking, empathy, and compassion.

4. The Pons, where a lot of regulatory neurotransmitters are produced.

The amygdala (fight or flight/anxiety and stress) part of the brain got smaller in this group, resulting in reduced stress levels.

This data shows changes in the brain after just eight weeks.

In this program, the subjects took one weekly class and were told to practice 40 minutes a day at home. The meditation recording was provided. That's it.

Again, mindfulness is just like exercise. It's a mental exercise. And just as any exercise increases health, helps us handle stress better, and promotes longevity, meditation can give us a balanced and healthy brain. [2]

Meditation and mindfulness are not cure-alls, but at the very least they should be filed under "Can't Hurt." They will absolutely help. They're just as useful as an adjunct therapy and as a standalone. And if nothing else, they put into your daily consciousness that you want to feel better and be better. It's like tying a string around your thumb to remember a task. This act reminds the brain – and your brain activity will change for the better based on that practice.

14

No Have-To's, No Right Or Wrong

I want to emphasize that you don't have to meditate for a certain number of minutes, or with your eyes closed. Start with 1-3 minutes like I did. Get comfortable with that. Think of something you want to manifest in your life. See people and situations you want in your life. Recall truly happy or joy-filled memories. If you have children, imagine them protected in a golden light as they go through their day and their lives. Sit with a cup of coffee overlooking your world and smile. Hum your favorite song. It relaxes the brain. Do the deep breathing – in deep and slow through your nose and out audibly through the mouth. Do it three times. This breathing physiologically relaxes the body. Go to your truly happy, contented place that I kind of tricked you into before. Breathe in. Breathe out. Think of your favorite color, or whatever color pops into your mind. Breathe in this color. Imagine, if this color were a person, what kind of person would they be?

What are the characteristics of this color person? What is a good day for them like? How do they act kindly?

This is another example of relaxing your brain. Let your mind make up a nice story about someone. See where it takes you. Make it positive and imagine all the good qualities about this color person. Imagine breathing in this color and all its good qualities.

See how you feel after you do this. I bet you'll feel better, lighter, maybe more patient.

Every doctor, parent, paramedic in the world knows that deep breathing relaxes the body. How often have we seen this mimicked on television? When the stressed-out person is being told by the doctor to breathe, breathe deep. That breathing is the in-through-the-nose-out-through-the-mouth breathing I've been talking about.

The brain is an amazing thing. It's designed to adapt constantly. World-renowned neuroscientist Richie Davidson at the <u>Center for Healthy Minds</u> at the University of Wisconsin-Madison, puts forth these three basic tenets:

1) You can train your brain to change
2) That change is measurable
3) New ways of thinking can change it for the better

Practicing mindfulness is not a quick fix, but it's worth a try. Practice it for a few minutes every day for a week and see how you feel. Try it as an experiment. If you generally feel better, try it for 5-7 minutes a day. The brain keeps changing, throughout our lives. This is great news because just like we practice something to learn it, we can practice happiness and cultivate it much the same way.

Remember my recurring nightmare? I did that all by my itty-bitty self without any studies or neuroimaging or PhDs. I retrained my brain. I made it a habit to write down one thing from my dream until I was remembering it in full. I was then able to change the course of the nightmare. That's pretty powerful, if I do say so myself.

But I had to practice remembering my dreams to get to the golden ring. The same holds true for training your brain to remember the positive and allow the areas of your brain that capture positive memories to grow and breathe and get strong.

Dr. Richardson says, "By focusing on wholesome thoughts, and directing our intentions in those ways, we can potentially influence the plasticity of our brains and shape them in ways that can be beneficial. That leads us to the inevitable conclusion that qualities like warm-heartedness and well-being should best be regarded as skills."

Neuroscientists are beginning to see that even short amounts of practice, like 30 minutes of meditation per day, can induce measurable changes in the brain that can be tracked on a brain scanner.

I found research to support 12 minutes of meditation a day, but I benefitted as soon as I started my 1-2 minute meditations.

It is decision plus practice to get you to actually live in your happy place all the time.

15

Beyond The Brain Bennys

Earlier studies on the benefits of yoga and meditation involved questionnaires and volunteer participation, so the results can be construed as somewhat subjective. Only recently have neuroimaging and genomics technology been used by scientists to measure physiological changes in greater detail.

John Denninger, a psychiatrist at Harvard Medical School, started a five-year study in 2010 on how yoga and meditation affect genes and brain activity in the chronically stressed. His work in early 2013 shows how these mind-body techniques can switch on and off genes linked to stress and immune function.

"There is a true biological effect," said Denninger, who is also the director of research at the Benson-Henry Institute for Mind Body Medicine at Massachusetts

General Hospital, one of Harvard Medical School's teaching hospitals. "The kinds of things that happen when you meditate do have effects throughout the body, not just in the brain."

Stress-induced conditions can include everything from hypertension and infertility to depression and even aging. They account for 60 to 90 percent of doctor's visits in the U.S., according to the Benson-Henry Institute. The World Health Organization estimates stress costs U.S. companies at least $300 billion a year through absenteeism, turnover, and low productivity. These findings are prompting many doctors to embrace alternative methods for reducing stress or recommending meditation as part of an overall health program.

Meditation devotees include Bill George (board member of Goldman Sachs Group and Exxon Mobil Corp.), Jerry Seinfeld, Rupert Murdoch, Kobe Bryant, Jeff Bridges, Clint Eastwood, Rick Goings (CEO of

Tupperware), Martin Scorsese, Howard Stern, Oprah Winfrey, and more. Now, those are all some pretty busy people, and they manage to make the time for meditation. They are not millionaires sitting on their money wondering what to do with their days; they are extremely busy and need to make time to relax their brains.

Mind-body medicine such as meditation was actually first pioneered by Harvard professor Herbert Benson in the late 1960s, paving the way for Denninger to test its effects on alleviating depression – in tandem with appropriate pharmaceuticals.

Denninger's study, which concluded in 2015, tracked over 200 healthy subjects with high levels of reported chronic stress for six months. One group of 70 participants practiced Kundalini yoga, another 70 meditated, and the rest listened to stress education audiobooks, all for 20 minutes a day at home. Kundalini is a form of yoga that incorporates meditation, breathing exercises, and the singing of mantras in addition to postures. It was chosen for the study because of its strong meditation component.

Unlike earlier studies, this was one of the first to focus on participants with high levels of stress specifically. The published study (PloS, May 2013) showed that one session of relaxation-response practice was enough to enhance the expression of genes involved in energy metabolism and insulin secretion and reduce expression of genes linked to inflammatory response and stress. There was an effect even among novices who had never practiced before.

BOOM! Should I drop the mic and walk out?

No. Because Harvard isn't the only place where scientists have started examining these benefits.

Scientists at the University of California at Los Angeles and Nobel Prize winner Elizabeth Blackburn found that 12 minutes of daily yoga meditation for eight weeks increased telomerase activity by 43 percent, suggesting an improvement in stress-induced aging. Blackburn shared the Nobel medicine prize in 2009 with Carol Greider and Jack Szostak for research on the telomerase "immortality enzyme," which slows the cellular aging process.

Twelve minutes. That's it. Twelve minutes a day to reduce stress to a noticeable degree in mind and body and *slow the aging process*. That means you could not only feel younger and more vibrant, but you can actually start to *look* noticeably younger.

Now I'm dropping the mic.

16

Forgiveness

We've all had injustices in our lives. We've all experienced sadness and loss and trauma. When we spend energy justifying our anger about this, it keeps our brains in that negative place. If we hold back forgiveness, what does that do to us? One, it keeps us from moving forward. For example, if you've gone through a break-up or divorce, and your partner or spouse was unfaithful, that level of anger and betrayal can literally be crippling your ability to move forward into a loving, totally fulfilling partnership. It's justified anger, is it not? They cheated. They were unfaithful. They destroyed the marriage. I was the best thing that ever happened to them and how dare they? Your family and friends will support you in this – for a little while. Anger is like a big block of ice all around you that keeps you frozen in place. It's with you when you embark on another relationship, whispering its negativity in your ear, subtly but surely directing your actions.

Here's the thing though. Forgiveness is never for the other person; it is always for you. Always.

I'll share something else with you.

I was date raped in college. It was our third date. I was an intern and he was a full-time employee. I noticed him. Tall, broad, nice smile. Handsome. Older. I smiled at him. I got him to notice me. I flirted with him. He asked me out for drinks. Then he asked me to dinner. We went to a comedy show in the area. It was our third date. I liked to wear short skirts and high heels. I still do. I was twenty years old at the time. I was not a virgin. I liked to party and drink and flirt and have a good time. I invited him up after this third date. I wanted to be able to make out with him in private. I was attracted to him. I was not planning on having sex. However, he overpowered me. I tried to explain to him that I didn't want to do this. He said awful things to me I will never forget. He slapped me in the face when I tried to resist. I stopped resisting after that. I was scared and crying. I let him do it so it would be over that much sooner.

I was ashamed, scared, and angry.

I did not tell anyone for a very, very long time. As I began my healing journey, I found it hard to forgive him. Who could blame me, right? He didn't deserve my forgiveness. He was a bad man. But what was it doing to me? How was it affecting my subsequent relationships with men? How was it affecting my own sense of self-worth and esteem? These feelings were locked into my brain and I was motivated from that point – whether I was aware of that or not. (I was not aware of it.) I repressed the event and kept it to myself.

It affected my relationships with men for a very long time.

So how did I forgive him? I meditated on it. Actually, I meditated on myself. I saw myself surrounded in golden light. Strong and smart. Not afraid to embrace my sexuality. Not afraid to give and accept love.

It took a while. Then I saw him in a golden light. I imagined myself releasing him into the sky and letting him float away. It took practice. Years after it happened, I was able to let it truly go.

Awakenings and feelings of awareness are not like lightning bolts; they are slow dawning realizations. There was no voice of God or rainbows in the sky. There was no one day I can pinpoint as the day I let it go. I just realized one day that I had. I felt a freer sense of strength about myself, strength I had been strangling with my repressed fear.

Remember how the brain works. It is programmed to remember the negative and, unless we balance out the negative with the positive, we are, as the saying goes, "doomed to repeat it."

By that I do not mean experiencing the same exact trauma over and over, but if we trap trauma in our brains, and do nothing to counteract it, we are motivated from that point subconsciously. My subconscious led me to men that were not appropriate partner material nor were they trustworthy or deserving of my love and affection. It reinforced the negativity associated with men that was trapped in my brain.

17

Ohmmm My God

The breathing in Kundalini yoga – which is
the breathing you did earlier, and the
breathing health professionals use to relax
traumatized patients – and meditation are
tools that can not only enable us to swim
smoothly in difficult waters but feel better
and look younger.

I started with the breathing first.

It's easy. Breathe in deep through the mouth
so that your chest and belly expand, and out
audibly through the mouth. This is actually
the way we breathed as babies, so you
already know how to do this.

Let's talk a minute about the chanting.
Chanting gets a bad rep. I find it peaceful,
and I feel as though it connects me to my
progenitors through the ancestral brain.
Remember that OM was used before there
was any formal music or singing. I love to

sing. I love songs that move me. So I equate the sound of OM with the ancient music of those before me.

It's a sound that Hindus and Buddhists regard as sacred, and its symbol was found in medieval manuscripts, temples, monasteries, etc. History indicates that OM is the first sound of creation. When we say it, we pause at the end on the M. I like to feel how the M vibrates on my lips.

A little more on OM:
The sound of OM encompasses all words, all sounds in human language. OM is a matrix of all sounds, so in its diversified form, AUM, it gives rise to all words used in language. All audible sounds are produced in the space within the mouth beginning at the root of the tongue and ending at the lips. The throat sound is A, and M is the lip sound, while the sound U represents the rolling forward of speech articulation which starts at the root of the tongue, continuing until it ends in the lips. To pronounce OM correctly, remember, the sound vibration is

pronounced "om" as in home.

AUM and OM: In Sanskrit, the sound "O" is a diphthong spelled "AU". As a result, the difference between OM and AUM is simply one of transliteration.

AUM represents the 3 Fold Division of Time:

      A – is the waking state

      U – is the dream state

      M – is the state of deep sleep

At the end of AUM is a pause, a silence. This represents the state known as Turiya, or Infinite Consciousness.

 The visual symbol represents the meaning of AUM.

The large bottom curve symbolizes the waking state, A.

The middle curve signifies the dream state, U.

The upper curve denotes the state of deep sleep, M.

The dot signifies the fourth state of

consciousness, Turiya.

The semicircle at the top represents Maya and separates the dot from the other three curves. It signals to us that it is the illusion of Maya that is an obstacle to realization of the Highest.

OM is associated with Ganesha; the physical form of <u>Lord Ganesha</u> is said to be that of OM. The upper curve of OM is identified with the head or the face of Ganesh. The Lower curve his belly. The twisted curve on the right side of OM is the trunk.[4]

That's a lot of OM, I know. But if you've read it this far, it's speaking to you. This can be a private practice. You do not have to tell anyone unless you become comfortable with it. Like I said, I started doing it in my car on the way to work. Then I started doing it on the way home. Then I took it to bed with me. I slept better and more deeply. I awoke refreshed and alert. I was never a morning person before I practiced daily meditation.

I don't always incorporate the word OM. I found a plethora of meditations. Meditations for manifesting, for abundance, for love – there's a meditation for nearly everything. And once you start investigating, you'll find the music and the words that speak to you.

18

Follow Your Heart

I mentioned heart wall removal. It's a real thing. First of all, the heart generates 60 to 1000 times more power and electromagnetic energy than our brains, making it the most powerful organ we have.

Our hearts beat about 100,000 times a day, 40 million times a year, and if the connections between our brains and our hearts were to be severed, our hearts would keep right on beating.

The electrocardiogram machine (EKG) was developed in 1895. Some of you may have seen or experienced electrodes glued to the chest while the machine produces a graph of the heartbeat. Certainly you've seen it in enough medical shows if not a real life experience.

Not too long ago, the magnetocardiogram (MCG) was developed to measure the magnetic field of the heart, rather than the electrical field. Scientists found that the heart's magnetic field extends up to twelve feet in diameter around the body. [6]

Twelve feet around the body!

Using the MCG, scientists have uncovered some other interesting findings:
- Every beat of the heart sends messages to all the cells of the body
- The brain in your head obeys the messages sent by the heart
- The heart can "think" for itself
- The heart has the ability to "remember" things

What does it mean? Well, for one, many scientists believe the heart is a "second brain." Some heart transplant recipients have reported new affinities, memories, and ethics from the donor along with the new heart.

For example:
- A 47-year-old Caucasian male received a heart from a 17-year-old African-American male. The recipient was surprised by his

newfound love of classical music. He discovered later that the donor, who loved classical music and played the violin, had died in a drive-by shooting, clutching his violin case to his chest.

- Paul Oldam, a lawyer from Milwaukee, received the heart of a 14-year-old boy and inherited a strange new craving for Snickers.

- A seven-year-old girl had recurring nightmares about being killed after receiving the heart of another child who had been murdered. Her descriptions of the murderer as well as the murder weapon led to the arrest and conviction of the killer.

Okay – the Snickers story may not be the most compelling argument, but the last one pretty much got me.

What is a Heart-Wall? Most of us have felt a "heartache" in the physical sense. Pressure or discomfort in the chest and throat occurs when the deepest part of us is under assault, typically when someone is hurting us or when we are feeling a deep sense of grief, hurt, or loss.

Heart-wall practitioners believe that the heart is the core of our being. And in fact, it is. And if this core part of us is under assault, and it happens more than a few times in our lives, the subconscious mind – as we have discussed before – forms defense mechanisms and emotional survival tactics that create an "energy wall" or a "force field" to protect from future heartache or grief. It is this energy that I believe is created in tandem with the heart and the brain, which forms an "energy wall", otherwise known as the "Heart-Wall."[5]

Think about this for a moment. There is a communication taking place between all of us, all the time. The human heart is both a sender of information and a receiver of information. The heart is a sender of the energy that we call "love," and a receiver of that same energy.

Consider this scenario for a moment. A child is born into a family in which one parent is volatile, angry, and emotionally or physically abusive. This child experiences this behavior on a regular basis. Eventually that child learns, usually instinctively, to put up a "wall" around themselves to protect against unpredictable or violent behavior. Over time, the layers of walls build up, making it difficult to feel things deeply, deal with any emotionally charged situation effectively, and even result in isolation and depression.

Another discovery shows that, when a person feels love or affection for another person, the *heartbeat* of the person sending that love or affection becomes measurable in the magnetic brain waves of the recipient. Studies also show that when two people in love meet up, their heartbeats actually begin to synchronize their beats to match each other.

Measurable. So all that "two hearts beat as one" stuff is actually true and can be measured.

WOW.

My years of sorrow during my IVF cycles created a huge heart wall. Similarly, the date rape episode in college traumatized me. Both because of the act itself and because I repressed the fear, rage, and shame of the event for many years. As I've said, it affected my relationships for years to come, and I had a hard time trusting men. It also resulted in a deep-seated feeling of unworthiness, which could have affected my ability to believe I would conceive a child and carry it to term.

Although I wanted to fall in love and be in love, those energies were effectively blocking my brain and my heart, and I selected relationships that were not loving nor would they grow to be. They were "safe" for me because my heart could not get hurt at that level again. It kept me safe from experiencing loss again. It also kept any man from really understanding me, and the wheels on that bus went around and round.

There are pages and pages of testimonials I could include here on people who had their heart walls removed and are now living fully, happy lives. Lives that are not without pitfalls and sorrows, but now those pitfalls and sorrows are dealt with appropriately, not with isolation and depression.

So, the big picture here is that we are trying to release trapped negative emotions, which are held in because of the walls built around them. I recommend a book called *The Emotion Code* by Bradley Nelson. It contains the simplest, most efficient method of releasing trapped emotions ever devised. It is easily learned by anyone, without any previous training. The release is permanent, and it works for all ages.

Picture negative emotions like hands strangling the brain and blocking the heart. The longer they are there, the thicker they become. When we release trapped emotions, we are setting our hearts and minds free – free to be happy and positive – and when we are happy and positive, we are that much more likely to reach our potentials.

We have heart energies that can now be measured. This is exciting stuff! The heart and the brain are approximately 12-14 inches apart. Yet it can be a long journey to bring these two together to act in tandem. The heart remembers things the brain cannot explain, because it is the heart that can survive without the brain. The walls we erect around our hearts – consciously or subconsciously – affect our actions and behaviors especially as they pertain to emotionally charged situations, and we must, if we want to be truly happy, examine these walls, accept the pain, and release it.

19

Halo Energy

Ever walk into a room with two people in it and know you've walked into the middle of an argument or other emotional conflict? Maybe you look from one person to the other and ask, "What's going on?"

You know something is going on without anyone saying a word. It's the energy in the room speaking to you – perhaps to the lizard brain which is assessing the level of danger and subsequent fight or flight response.

But you knew something was going on seconds before you stepped into the room. That's the energy of those beings speaking to your energy. And before the logical mind has a chance to process, the intuitive/primal brain asks what's going on.

I call this halo energy. It's like turning off a light bulb: does the room go immediately

pitch black, or does the last of the light
slowly fade?

You know this energy. It can also manifest in
the form of nonverbal communication.
When we trust our intuitions more, and tap
into the energies around us, most of us
would be amazed at how accurate our
findings are.

20

Off The Beaten Path

I'm going to talk briefly about other methods of clearing out and tapping in. First, let's acknowledge that we all have had negative experiences and, from those, some trapped negative emotions about certain subjects. What I think we do not acknowledge enough is how those negative experiences and trapped emotions create our energy.

I sought out methods of healing. I retrained my brain to think a certain way. But my heart still needed work.

These methods are not for everyone, I merely list them as part of my experience and my journey to happiness.

Soul Retrieval is a Shamanic practice that believers feel is the most important level healing in spirit or energy work.

The beliefs behind this ancient practice include that once the spiritual energy has been intruded and damaged, it creates tears or holes in the person's fabric that allows further intrusions; therefore, the holes must be healed.

We all have ancestors that hunted if we go back far enough. Soul retrieval calls upon these hunters in our DNA to track the lost parts of our souls. The shamanic practitioner joins with the helping spirits to return the soul parts to the person in question and restore the energy matrix to its original, whole state.

Very often a soul part has found refuge in a lower world, meaning it is often being cared for by an animal spirit. A soul part in the middle world might be protected by an ancestor, and a soul part in the upper world may be held by a guardian angel.

The shaman's process is much like that of traditional western practitioners, in that they first identify the nature of the illness. The next step is where the divergence occurs. The shaman can empower the person, while in an expanded state of consciousness (remember the AM/FM radio analogy?) and neutralize them at spiritual and energetic levels, preventing any reoccurrence. Shamans call upon the compassionate forces just beyond the borders of our physical world to help. [7]

Stay with me. I know this is easily dismissed. Almost every doctor you know has witnessed a medical miracle that they cannot explain by science or medical expertise. Doctors have told me that medical science can only go so far and then God takes over.

I personally believe in angels. I have been in some horrific situations in my life and was led out of them without incident or damage. I have been careless in my life. I have drunk to excess many times. There were times – in one state of inebriation or another – that I actually felt prevented from going into that room, or into that car, or down that alley. In an inebriated state, I think we all know that the logical brain is not functioning properly, leaving room for the intuitive to take over.

Let me share an example with you. My sister is very pragmatic. She is a skilled attorney and mediator. She has always been this way. And while she loves that I have this very open, spiritual side of me, it is not a practice she embraces for herself. That's fine. But when she was overseas for a semester abroad in college, she and her best friend got completely wasted in a bar. They met a nice-looking young man about their age who told them about a party around the corner. They agreed to go, stumbling together down the street, laughing. The young man turned into a break between two buildings as a shortcut and waved them in. It was a short dark alley.

As my logical, pragmatic sister tells it, she took one step into that alley and she felt like she slammed into a brick wall. Her hand went to her forehead immediately where she felt she had hit it, and she grabbed her friend and they ran in the other direction.

Who knows what lay beyond that step? Who knows if this nice-looking college-aged man they were drinking and laughing with had bad intentions? But she believed to her core that there was danger there. Something stopped her. Intuition? Guardian angel? Ancestor? It doesn't really matter. What matters is that her inebriated state allowed her logical brain to shut down, and her intuitive brain was open to messages – from either herself or a spirit.

Understand that I am not making a case for public inebriation, rather a case for the intuitive; some people just need a little help to get to that place.

I think all of us have experienced something...otherworldly. The day my father died, I was on my way to the hospital. He had been hospitalized twice that year for things that turned out not to be serious. I did not know that this was the day he would die. As I was locking my door, planning to go to work after I had seen him, I heard his voice tell me to not forget that he wanted "Wild Colonial Boy" played on bagpipes at his funeral. Before my logical brain could process this, I said, "I know Dad, I remember", out loud and vaguely annoyed. Then I started to cry, because I knew. I knew today was the day. My logical brain fought against it, but my heart knew. And such was the case.

Who doesn't have a good ghost story to tell? Some unexplainable-by-logic incident?

If we are open to it, the universe is constantly streaming messages to us. Repeated numbers like 222, 333, and 444 all have angelic messages. If we notice these things, we are noticing them for a reason. Something as simple as almost falling or tripping is a little message to me to watch my step that day, either literally or in my dealings with people.

The day after my friend Suzan died, a butterfly landed on my shoulder. It was the first time that ever happened to me. My brain can dismiss that as odd. But my heart swelled and my eyes filled with tears because I knew it was her telling me she was okay.

A week after my dad died, I found three pennies on my white kitchen floor. I'm pretty neat, and I have a jar in which I put all my change. Copper pennies are fairly noticeable on a white floor. They were not there the previous morning and they were not there that night. I would have stepped on them while doing the dishes and at least felt the cold metal under my feet. Three is my favorite number and I was born in the third month of the year. I knew it was Dad. Before I could process it, tears sprang to my eyes and my heart rate increased – all involuntary actions.

Now when I find a penny somewhere, I say hi to my Dad, and I thank him for letting me know he watches over me.

Let's look at the concept of the spirit animal for a minute. All animals have specific qualities assigned to them. Dreaming about them or having them noticeably appear in your life can be a message relevant to what is going on in your life. You can Google the animal you dreamed about – like 'dog spirit animal' and see what it says. I'd bet that the qualities associated with this animal have direct relevance to your life.

My brother often smells my grandfather. He occasionally hears my father's footsteps walking along the side of his house to the back door, coming in for a beer on a Sunday afternoon, like he often did. Here's the thing: intuition, true intuition, is a surprise. Some people call them 'a-ha' moments – when suddenly a long-time situation becomes clear, and we can't believe we didn't see it before. Some people, like my brother, simply accept it.

21

Open Up!

A word on prayer. Most people believe in *some*thing. I believe in God. I was raised Catholic and although I don't subscribe to all the teachings of the Bible, I do believe in something larger and more powerful than myself.

Call it God, Zen, Buddha, Source, or anything you want. But when I need help with something, I pray. When I have a friend who needs help with something, I'll pray for them. I don't go to church all the time and light candles and pray on my rosary beads. Not that there is anything wrong with that. My prayers can be as simple as "I just need help right now." Sometimes I have to pray to accept a certain situation. Sometimes I pray for patience. (I pray for it to hurry up – ba-dump-cha.) And if I am praying for patience, do you know what happens? I do not get automatically patient. Not at all. I am then placed in horrific traffic when I am already late to work and I have a meeting with my boss that I am now going to miss. I am placed in situations that require patience, so I can practice it. Like everything else in this book. Changing something requires practice.

One of my favorite stories is that of the man and the butterfly. A man is walking along a meadow one day and he sees a butterfly struggling to get out of its cocoon. He stops and helps the butterfly, releasing it from the cocoon so it can fly free. The man feels good about this as he watches the butterfly fly. After a few flits of the wings, though, the butterfly falls to the ground and dies. The man asks God: why? Why did you let that butterfly die after I helped him? God tells the man: because the butterfly needs the struggle of getting out of the cocoon to develop the muscles to fly.

Look at the difficult or challenging situations in your life. What did you learn or are you in the process of learning? If we are struggling with something, we probably already know the answer to that problem; we just don't want to act on it the way we know we should. Maybe the result of taking that action feels scary or unfamiliar, so we stay in it. We suffer through it, trying to fix something or someone. The key here is that if you are struggling with a decision or a situation, there is a part of it you are not accepting as reality.

I've done that a lot in my life. I've stayed in relationships long past their expiration date – and it's no one's fault. Sometimes the only thing left standing between two people is the truth. Sometimes relationships and situations run their course, and they were in our lives to teach us something, to develop our muscles for the next thing. To bring us to the place where we are supposed to fly. To bring us to the people with whom we are supposed to fly.

In keeping with the butterfly metaphor, change can be scary at first, messy in the middle, and transformative at the end.

Transformative. It's such a good word.

I am happy. I have a very positive outlook on life. Everything does not go smoothly. I have challenges and frustrations just like everyone else. I do not have everything in my life that I want. But I am happy. I want to stay happy. I want the people I care about to be happy.

It takes practice.

22

Chakra Science

The great Nikola Tesla is credited with this saying: *"The day science begins to study non-physical phenomena, it will make more progress in one decade than in all the previous centuries of its existence."*

With that in mind, I'd like to add in some history and science about the chakras. For those of you who accept these tenets, you can skip this chapter and go straight to Chapter 23.

The word *chakra* is defined as a spinning disk or wheel. On the human body, the chakra is a spinning disk of energy that runs along the spine. Many Eastern health practitioners believe that the health of one's chakra is directly connected to the health of the physical body, the mind, and emotional wellbeing of a person.

The chakra system dates back to 1500-500 BC, India, from an ancient text known as the

Vedas. In this book are revelations seen by ancient sages after intense meditation that have been carefully preserved since that times.

Most of you know that all matter is held together via energetic bonds, and the movement of energy is vital to life. When we think, breathe, function, or rest, electrical energy is flowing through our bodies via our neurons and nerve pathways. Ok. That's a given.

What's interesting about the chakras is how the position of the major chakras corresponds to major nerve 'plexus' or nerve 'bundles' in our bodies – and how their placements run along the length of the spine.

What came first? Chakra alignment or the discovery of glands in our bodies that correlate to these chakra points? Electrophotonic analysis in medicine is used to understand and measure the effectiveness of Ancient Eastern Mysticism – and it's a practice that has been gaining more attention from scientists and researchers all over the world. In the mid-90s, Konstantin Korotkov, Professor of Computer Science and Biophysics at Saint-Petersburg Federal University, developed the GDV, a scientific device based on the ancient Chinese system of energy meridians. The GDV measures the bioenergy of living organisms, as well as the environment, and it provides evaluation that can highlight potential health (physiological and psycho-emotional) abnormalities.

Back to the chakras. Our chakras are positioned into the spinal column at various locations beginning with the coccyx, rising all the way to the crown of the head. Dr. Pradeep B. Deshpande, a Professor Emeritus at the Department of Chemical Engineering at the University of Louisville, explains that each chakra resonates at a different frequency level. "With new BioWell software, it is now possible to quantitively estimate the energy of the chakras, graphically display their level of activation, and indicate whether this level of activation is above or below the level found from large numbers of subjects."

The results from a case study he conducted involving over 100 participants in attendance indicate that imbalanced Chakras are easily detectable:

"Each individual sector or portion of the fingertip is connected energetically with specific organs and organ systems such as the respiratory system. When the data of the 10 individual BIO-grams are collated and interpolated, an image of the entire full body energy field is created. The gaps and the reduced emissions and out-of-balance Chakras for the unhealthy individual are quite obvious."[9]

Energy cannot be seen with the naked human eye, which is why attempts to measure our invisible force fields are often met with disdain or criticism. However, the groundbreaking work of dedicated scientists all over the world has opened a door to the mainstream acceptance of the non-material science. I'm referring to the idea that what we perceive as physical material is not the only reality available for us to study – and great strides have been made to do so.

We talked about measuring heart energy as our hearts emit electromagnetic fields which change according to our emotions and we can now measure this magnetic field up to twelve feet around the body. We now have documented proof that positive emotions create physiological benefits in our bodies and conjuring up positivity can boost the immune system. Conversely, negative emotions can create nervous system chaos that is counteracted by the effects of positive emotions. So feelings of love, gratitude, and compassion – any positive feelings whatsoever – have a larger impact than we could have ever imagined.

Here's how it's measured: A completely painless electrical current is applied to the fingertips to measure the body's response in the form of an "electron cloud" which is composed of light energy photons. The glow of this discharge is invisible to the human eye, as humans can only see one percent of the entire electromagnetic spectrum. It is captured by an optical CCD camera system and translated into a digital computer.

In the GDV software programs, the glow from the different sectors of the finger images is projected onto the shape of a human body in correspondence with the locations of the different organs and systems. As a result, we can see energy field images that allow for intuitive analysis of the physiological level of human body functioning.

So while we can measure energy fields, the interpretation still requires intuition. However, this process has been approved and received registration as a routine medical diagnostic device by the Russian Ministry of Health upon recommendation of the Russian Academy of Sciences.

Now. How this correlates to the chakra centers on our bodies. According to Eastern metaphysical theories of Ayurvedic Indian medicine, there are seven chakras or integrated energy centers that are widely believed to be correlated with physical, mental, emotional, and spiritual wellbeing. These energy chakras are positioned or embedded into the spinal column at various locations beginning with the coccyx, rising all the way to the crown of the head.

"Each chakra is considered to resonate at a different frequency level. With new BioWell software, it is now possible to quantitatively estimate the energy of chakras and graphically display their level of activation and indicate whether this level of activation is above or below the level found from large numbers of subjects," found Dr. Pradeep B. Deshpande, a professor emeritus at the Department of Chemical Engineering at the University of Louisville.

Dr. Deshpande had over 100 participants in attendance for a study in these energy centers. Clinical studies of more than 10,000 patient cases encompassing various health challenges have also been well documented in Russia.

The graphic showed aligned chakras, indicating that the subject was calm, relaxed and nourished, after meditation, breathing practices, and energies on love, kindness and intention. A smoothing of the energy field before and after the case study was also observed. Results like this were consistent among a large number of volunteers.

A healthy and balanced emotional state is correlated with truthfulness, honesty, steadfastness, equanimity, unconditional love, compassion, gratitude, the ability to discern truth from falsehood, spontaneous affection, and the capacity to remain calm despite what's occurring in the external world. An unhealthy and emotionally unbalanced state is correlated with attachment, ego, greed, lying, fear, anger, irritation, sorrow, and more.

This is another example of how consciousness is directly correlated with our physical world, with regards to health and much more. As we've already discussed earlier in this book, there are many scientific studies that prove consciousness can alter our material circumstances.

'Everything is energy' is a widely accepted theory in quantum physics and a scientifically proven fact. In religion and spirituality, the movement of energy is the central and fundamental core around which many traditions are based. Ancient practices such as Reiki, QiGong, and Tai Chi focus on the manipulation of energy to achieve wellbeing.

Remember: a lot of these ancient traditions derive from primitive understandings of biology and a degree of flexibility is necessary when trying to understand their significance.

The most energetic processes within our bodies are caused by our nerve tissues and specifically our nervous systems. The nervous system coordinates *voluntary* and *involuntary* actions and transmits signals to and from different parts of the body and brain. It is the communication hub of the body.

The nervous system is composed of two main parts: The Central Nervous System (CNS) within the brain and spinal cord, and the Peripheral Nervous System (PNS), which connects the brain and spinal cord to the rest of the body, via small river-like nerve fibers. This system is what correlates with the chakras.

There are different categories of nerve bundles within the PNS, but the most relevant to the chakras is the autonomic nervous system of the PNS. This deals with the involuntary or automatic responses within the body, e.g. digestion, heart rate, sneezing, swallowing, and breathing. All these processes are regulated by the hypothalamus.

The Autonomic Nervous System is further divided into the Sympathetic Nervous System (activated in emergencies to move energy, the *'fight and flight'* responses) and the Parasympathetic Nervous system (activated when *'resting and digesting'*).

It is the Parasympathetic Nervous System which has the greatest relevance to the areas where the chakras are thought to be located.

The diagrams below show where these major nerve plexus (or networks) of the Parasympathetic Nervous System lie. The brain connects to these parts of the body via the vagus nerve – the 10th cranial nerve and pretty much the holy grail of all nerves. Where the major networks of nerves are, they correspond with the glands in our bodies.

The diagram below shows the position of the various chakras. Notice how they correlate to the PNS diagram on the right.

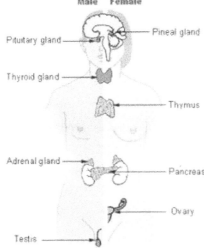

So why do glands require so much electrical input? Glands secrete hormones into the bloodstream and are extremely important in the functioning of our bodies. They require energy to do that. Just as food or drink is turned into energy of the body, our Vagus nerve points/chakras need energy for their own balance and proper function.

Hormones are critical players in the body's chemistry and stimulated by the Vagus nerve. They (along with nerves) carry messages between cells and organs and affect many aspects of our bodily processes, from growth through childhood, sexual development, mood, to how well we sleep, how we manage stress, brain functioning, and even how we break down food. In fact, the gradual decrease in hormone production over time is what ages us. Other hormones, such as DMT (Dimethyltryptamine), secreted by the pineal gland in the brain, are known to cause out of body experiences, heightened creativity, and even psychic abilities.

The chakras are associated with the major nerve networks within the body, which connect the brain/spine, via the major Vagus nerve, to the glands responsible for hormone production and the functioning of the body in general. The Vagus nerve mostly conveys sensory information about the state of the body's organs to the Central Nervous System. Once it leaves the brain, it winds its way down the body and around the internal organs.

One key role that the Vagus nerve plays is the 'reset' button, built in to counteract our internal, automatic, 'alarm' system, resulting in the fight and flight response – a key culprit in stress and depression.
Therefore, *stimulation* of the Vagus nerve may lead to some very positive health benefits, especially in someone suffering from the effects of subconscious fear (fear of stability, the status of our jobs, terrorist attacks, money, etc.).

The Kundalini Serpent

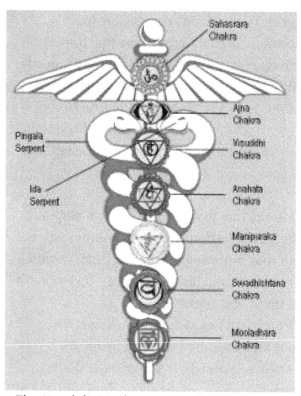

The Kundalini is the ancient description for the energy (or *shakti*) present within our bodies. It is said that the kundalini stems from the base of the spine and winds its way up to the top of the head, often compared to a snake or a serpent. 'Kundalini awakening'

is said to result in deep meditation, enlightenment, and deep sense of bliss. It is said that this Kundalini 'snake' coils 3 times as it travels up the spine. And guess what - the Vagus nerve connects precisely 3 times to the spine. Although the ancient descriptions may be considered a little far-fetched, it appears perhaps they used metaphors for very accurate information related to our well-being.

Notice how the Kundalini 'snake' looks much like the caduceus symbol for medicine.

There are over 13,000 studies on the Vagus nerve, and it is well-documented that Vagus Nerve Stimulation can assist in a multitude of illnesses, such as treatment-resistant depression and certain forms of epilepsy.

The most effective, natural method for stimulating the Vagus nerve? Deep belly breathing.

Some documented Advantages of Vagus Nerve Stimulation include:
Memory retention
Increased calm
Increased sense of bliss
Reduced blood pressure
Controlled respiration
Neuroplasticity
Improved immune system response
Reduced neural inflammation
Reduction in stress levels
Alleviation of depression
Treatment of certain types of epilepsy
Improved cognitive behavior

Quantum Physics has already proven that observation affects matter. Since all of matter is energy organized in a particular arrangement, perhaps the ancient traditions of observing thought or placing attention and awareness on the chakras, bear real weight. Especially when it comes to creating real changes within the body.

We've all seen and read instruction manuals. They show us how to build or install equipment. But first someone had to build that piece of equipment. Before that someone had to *think* of how to build it.

Consider the Great Pyramids of Giza — some of the most magnificent man-made structures in history. We can date these back to 305 BC during the Ptolemaic period and the massive scale reflects the role that the pharaoh, or king, played in ancient Egyptian society. More than 4,000 years later, the Egyptian pyramids still retain much of their majesty. *Four thousand years later.* Imagine a home lasting that long and imagine building it with no blueprint.

Stonehenge is another phenomenon. Dating back to 3100 BC, archaeologists believe it was built over the course of 1500 years using primitive tools to dig a massive circular henge (ditch) on Salisbury Plain.

Stonehenge's builders hoisted an estimated 80 non-indigenous bluestones, 43 of which remain today, into standing positions and placed them in either a horseshoe or circular formation. The largest weighs more than 40 tons and rises 24 feet. How, then, did prehistoric builders without sophisticated tools or engineering or any blueprint haul these boulders, which weigh up to 4 tons, over such a great distance and then stand them up?

Some scientists have suggested that glaciers, not humans, did most of the heavy lifting, and that the Earth is dotted with giant rocks known as glacial erratics that were carried over long distances by moving ice floes. Most archaeologists dismiss this theory, because how could nature deliver the exact number of stones needed to complete the circle?

The Brú na Bóinne in Ireland was also built as a sacred passage tomb/burial site built in 3300 BC. There were at least 40 passage tombs within the Newgrange structure. Not only that, but the passage and chamber are aligned with the rising sun at the Winter Solstice, so when the sun rises, the opening is perfectly aligned to fill the passageways with golden light. To this day, people all over the world gather here for the sunrise on the Winter Solstice.

All of these structures display a sophisticated knowledge of architecture, engineering, astronomy, carpentry, and craftsmanship.

How were these structures even conceived?

The people of that time called them visions; we call them ideas. What's the difference really? The people that conceived and built these structures were not formally taught in any educational setting. They were not conditioned to worship logic. They sat quietly and let the visions come to them. We did that earlier with the color person. You let your mind wander into the calm familiar landscape of your mind and let the story create itself.

When they hit a block, they sat and contemplated (another word for meditation) until the solution came to them. This not only supports the intuitive process but also demonstrates fascinating aspects of how the brain works – and how it *can* work. We limit our own belief systems and thereby limit our lives and ourselves. The people that built those structures were not limited because no limiting belief was ever placed on them. There was no test to say 'you're just not a numbers person' or any other limiting thought. They had the idea/vision and they went and did it.

Frankly, that's how most great success stories start.

The ancient healers of our world were not limited either. They went by instinct and intuition. Granted they had no choice, but discoveries made along the way greatly enabled these people to treat infections and other ailments.

The point is, the further we delve into our history, the more we discover. All medicine –

save for synthetic drugs which use man-made chemicals – is derived from some natural source – plant, minerals, soils, gases – and has since been reinvented over and over.

If we go back to the beginning, the first documented evidence of any kind of medicine or healing modalities started with energy. When someone's energy was low, or they were feverish, they called in a shaman or a medicine woman to identify and heal. Many people died of fevers and infections that more modern medicine could have helped. Many people were cleared and cured.

Penicillin was discovered by accident. In 1928, Alex Fleming (I remember this by his last name Fleming, as a cure for phlegm due to the common cold) was reviewing his petri dishes of varying bacteria when he saw one of them with a growing blob of mold. The bacteria immediately surrounding the mold had broken down — as if the mold had secreted something that inhibited bacterial growth. This mold proved to be capable of killing a wide range of harmful bacteria, such as streptococcus, meningococcus, and the diphtheria bacillus. The rest is history.

Again, it started with natural plants and minerals and intuitive thoughts. And while modern medicine has made great strides, there is still no cure for cancer. There is still no cure for brain-related diseases such as Parkinson's or Alzheimer's. Perhaps if we work in tandem with all we know about all treatments, and marry Eastern and Western philosophies, we can make great strides, just as Tesla suggested.

23

Chakra Explanation And Meditation

I am including a chakra meditation that I have used successfully on myself, on my friends, and as part of my Reiki healing practice.

We actually have thousands of chakras; however, I'm going to focus on the ten main chakras.

Our own bioenergy –the heart and brain waves each of us emit, as previously discussed – also known as chi, has vortexes called chakras. Chakras act as points of connection between our physical and non-physical (astral, extraphysical) bodies, enabling energies to flow from one of these vehicles of manifestation to the other. They are the vehicle by which we absorb and exchange energy to and from the environment; therefore, they form the core system through which we sustain our energy levels, vitality, and health.

Look at them like our personal energy devices, and because each chakra represents certain beliefs, awareness of the energies here are vital to our well-being.

The main way that chakras replenish their energies is through sleep. So even on an unconscious level, we experience a quasi-astral projection (out of body experience) when we sleep. Have you ever felt like you were flying or falling, and you wake up with a start, or gripping the edges of the bed? That's astral projection.

Our chakras, while having specific functions, are interconnected and work in harmony with the physical body. Consequently, an imbalance in one or more chakra energies can manifest physically: migraines, IBS, shortness of breath, digestion issues, back and joint pains, etc. Most imbalances are emotionally based.

It's important to first identify if there are physical root causes to any pain: a broken bone, old injuries, etc. If there are no physical realities, we look at the energy centers. For example, a block in the throat chakra energy could be caused by shock or grief. The person experiences chest tightness, pressure or a heat sensation in the throat or chest.

As we've already discussed, traumas can cause blockages in our hearts and brains. They can also cause energy imbalances and blocked energy centers. Our chakras can tell us where our strong points and weak points lie and help us understand how we couple conscious and unconscious energies in our own bodies.

A chakra practitioner can divine these energies through several methods. I like to take my clients through a relaxing meditation of seven to ten chakras in order to get the full picture. I work from instinct and from the feet up.

The feet chakras are at the soles of the feet. We absorb energy from the earth from these points which relates to our overall physical energy. There is also the root chakra, located at the base of the spine or the top of the pubic bone. As this relates to physical vitality, it also connects us to our sense of self and financial well-being. It is where fear of financial insecurity brews, and where we can release it to remove blockages to that. The color associated with these chakras is a deep, earthy red. Think of the times in your life when you were worried about or inordinately focused on money. Did your back ache? Maybe you dismissed it as sleeping funny, or working out too hard, but because this chakra is relevant to our financial footing, its imbalance can create pain in the back areas.

The next chakra is located below the belly button (and similarly the same area on the back – this is true for all torso chakras) and its color is orange. Here is where we house our sexual energies and our emotional relationships with family and deep friendships. In my experience, this is where most women hold grief. Just as regular sexual activity is important for maintaining healthy energies, irregular or dissatisfying relationships can result in bad or unmatched energies. This chakra on me was blocked for a long time since this is the area of reproductive organs as well as emotionally healthy sexual relationships. I've often seen women instinctively cover their sacral area with their hands when hearing sorrowful news.

The third chakra is the sacral chakra and it is located above the belly button. Its color is golden yellow. It is the core of our beings, our sense of value and personal success. It's also the area of survival instincts when facing danger – why we often get a pang in that area for a "low blow" or a "gut punch" in emotional conflicts or grief. Again, note the correlation to the energy we are receiving and the physical reaction. It is connected.

I usually go to the heart chakra next, but there is a spleen chakra that is closely related to the sex chakra. It's where we hold profound sadness and lack of fulfillment, so if there are issues, I work on that too.

The heart chakra is located between the lungs, and it absorbs energy accordingly. I find this area is more sensitive in men. An imbalance in this chakra can sometimes manifest as feeling heaviness or pressure in the chest despite no known physiological cause. Regular physical contact with the people we love helps to maintain its health and vitality. This is another area that people instinctively cover when hearing bad news, but that news is often more horrifying than sorrowful. These instinctual reactions, I believe, are wired into our ancestral DNA.

There are also palm chakras – which I rarely work with on clients but use frequently for my work –where we absorb and direct energy, so they are particularly effective if I need to locate a source of pain or discomfort. This discomfort presents itself as a heated area to my palms. They are also a good conduit if I need to "borrow" energy from any other chakra and direct it to affected areas.

The throat chakra is a pretty light blue color. It relates to our communication, speaking our truth, self-expression, and standing up for ourselves. If this area is blocked, there is usually something the person is not saying or not acknowledging regarding a personal emotional issue. Consider the term "lump in your throat" as the physical manifestation of this blockage. This also happens in periods of grief and mourning; we simply cannot find the words to express such grief. Likewise in cases of being shocked to the point of speechlessness.

The next one is again not something I work with often, but it relates to communications with non-physical consciousness (individuals who have passed away) and is at the back of the head near the cerebellum (base of the head and top of the spine). The cerebellum is the part that receives information from the sensory systems, the spinal cord, and other parts of the brain, and then regulates motor movements. Remember the cerebellum dance.

People with high levels of energetic sensitivity and enhanced intuition usually have a more activated or sensitive energy in this chakra.

The next chakra is my favorite. Not only because it's my favorite color, purple, but because it can activate and strengthen the intuition with which we are all born. My mother told me this story: when I was a child of three or four, I walked to where my mother was sitting, staring into space. I tugged at her sleeve and I said, "Don't worry Mommy. We're going to find a white house that has green shutters with little moons in them." She had in fact been stressing about buying a house, with my brother on the way, and was worried she and my father would not find something they could afford.

Three months later, my brother was a month old and we were moving into a new home. As we were unpacking the car, she says she picked me up and I said, "See, Mommy? Little moons in the shutters." Sure enough, the house was white with green shutters and the shutters had little half-moons in them.

As children we have not yet learned to dismiss intuition and we are almost completely intuitive. This is why babies know how to hold their breath underwater when they are first born; it's instinct/intuition.

Back to the chakra, this is our intuitive chakra, located between the eyebrows. A well-developed third eye chakra strengthens our extrasensory perceptions and facilitates the lucid projection. Some people experience sensations of pulsation, movement, contractions, etc. in the forehead when this area is activated. I often see people place their whole hand to their foreheads when faced with a problem, or fingers on their temples to think something through. Most of these movements are instinctual. Meditating on the color indigo here, surrounding your problem with this color, will relax the brain and allow it to access the creative centers for a solution.

Finally, there is the crown chakra. This is at the very top of the head and it related to the pituitary gland. It faces upward where the other chakras face out. It serves to activate the other chakras, and it is where we bring in divine messaging and protection. This is associated with the color white, but I like it to be a sparkly white with a lavender outline. Working on this area helps us trust the process, and even enhance retrocognition (recall of past lives) or precognition (forecast of future events or lives). Consider the phrase, "it's in the back of my head." We are instinctually calling upon this area of the brain to access the information. I believe this is where ancestral data lives as well.

For my meditation purposes, I go through the seven chakras: root (red), sacral (orange), solar plexus (golden yellow), heart (teal), throat (light blue), third eye (purple/indigo), and crown (sparkly white).

Let's try it.

Lie down and get comfortable, arms at your side. Wiggle your legs and arms and fingers and toes. Let your body feel supported by the bed or couch you are laying on. Close your eyes.

Picture the root chakra on your body – that's the bottoms of the feet and base of the spine/top of the pubic bone. Imagine the deep red color of this chakra like a circle the size of a quarter on your body. Picture this same color red light coming down from the sky and entering these circle points on your body. Imagine it spinning and balancing these energy areas. The mantra that you can say silently to yourself is *I have enough to share and enough to spare*. Say it three times. Breathe in this deep red light and imagine it spinning out counterclockwise from your body and joining streams with the same colored light from the sky. Breathe in deeply. See this chakra in perfect balance and harmony to your body and the universe.

Move your eyes to the next chakra – orange. Picture it on your body – below the belly button. Imagine the deep orange color of this chakra like a circle the size of a quarter on your body. Picture this same color orange light coming down from the sky and entering this circle point on your body. Imagine it spinning and balancing this energy area. The mantra that you can say silently to yourself is *I create loving relationships in my life*. Say it three times. Breathe in this deep orange light and imagine it spinning out counterclockwise from your body and joining streams with the same colored light from the sky. Breathe in deeply. See this chakra in perfect balance and harmony to your body and the universe.

Picture the next chakra on your body – above the belly button and below the sternum. Imagine the bright golden yellow color of this chakra like a circle the size of a quarter on your body. Picture this same color light coming down from the sky and entering this circle point on your body. Imagine it spinning and balancing this energy area. The mantra that you can say silently to yourself is *I am successful in all my undertakings.* Say it three times. Breathe in this beautiful golden light and imagine it spinning out counterclockwise from your body and joining streams with the same colored light from the sky. Breathe in deeply. See this chakra in perfect balance and harmony to your body and the universe.

Picture the next chakra on your body – the heart chakra in between your lungs. Imagine a deep, rich teal color – I like to see this as a rich paint stream coming down into this area. Picture this same deep teal color light coming down from the sky and entering your heart chakra. I like to see it inside my heart, the paint-like quality of it filling in all the cracks and breaks, healing the heart. Breathe deeply. Imagine a beautiful lotus flower opening in the middle of the rich teal. This is sacred. Your heart is sacred. Imagine it spinning and balancing this energy area. The mantra that you can say silently to yourself is *I create loving and supportive relationships in my life.* Say it three times. Breathe in this beautiful teal light and imagine it spinning out counterclockwise from your body and joining streams with the same colored light from the sky. Breathe in deeply. See this chakra in perfect balance and harmony to your body and the universe.

Next is the throat chakra. Picture the prettiest light blue of a summer sky. Picture this same vibrant light blue color coming down from the sky and entering your throat chakra. I like to see it wafting around inside my throat and back of my neck. Breathe deeply. Imagine it spinning and balancing this energy area. The mantra that you can say silently to yourself is *I communicate easily and effectively.* Say it three times. Breathe in this beautiful light and imagine it spinning out counterclockwise from your body and joining streams with the same colored light from the sky. Breathe in deeply. See this chakra in perfect balance and harmony to your body and the universe.

Next is the third eye chakra located between your eyebrows. This is a deep purple or indigo color. I like to place white and blue sparkles in it. Picture this same deep purple color coming down from the sky and entering your third eye chakra. I like to imagine it filling the inside of my head, circling around and relaxing all the areas of the brain. Calming, nurturing, allowing. Breathe deeply. Imagine it spinning and balancing this energy area. The mantra that you can say silently to yourself is *I listen to my intuition and allow and receive it in my daily life.* Say it three times. Breathe in this beautiful light and imagine it spinning out counterclockwise from your body and joining streams with the same colored light from the sky. Breathe in deeply. See this chakra in perfect balance and harmony to your body and the universe.

Last but definitely not least is the crown chakra on the top of your head. This is a sparkly white color with a lavender outline. Feel this powerful light of the source entering the top of your head. As it enters your head, imagine it streaming down through your entire body, gently gliding down your head and face, your neck and shoulders, your arms and fingers, your torso, your legs and calves and ankles and toes. Imagine it creates this white/lavender outline around your body as you lay there. On the deep breath in, imagine this outline seeping into your body; on the exhale, imagine it creating a glow around your body. Smile. This feels nice. Breathe deeply. Imagine this light weaving down to the root chakra and threading through the red root, looping around and threading through the orange chakra, the golden chakra, the teal chakra, the light blue chakra, the purple chakra, and finally to the crown chakra. I like to tie an imaginary knot in it - sealing in all the balanced chakras together as one.

Breathe in deeply. See yourself as you lie there – balanced and relaxed and happy. Smile. Breathe in. Breathe out.

Slowly wiggle your fingers and toes and move your body slightly. Slowly open your eyes. Smile. You are balanced and peaceful. All is well.

I hope you like the above meditation. I do it several times a week before bed. My wish for you is to be happy in all areas of your life: deeply happy and truly fulfilled.

24

What Does It All Mean?

A quick review of the energy centers in our bodies. Since each area represents physical characteristics of the body, I want to point out how imbalanced chakras can actually manifest.

The root chakra (red/base of spine, top of pubic bone) stands for our inherited beliefs developed in our formative years. It's also our identification with the physical world, finances, and careers. This is our grounding chakra, so when we are feeling financially unstable, we may experience pain or tightness in our lower or middle backs. Let's flip that around. Do you have or have you had lower back pain? What was happening in your life then? I'll wager there was some level of financial insecurity going on.

A damaged or imbalanced chakra will function much differently. If your 0-7 years were challenging and without love, you may experience survival issues like emotional dysfunction, stress, anxiety, and restlessness. This includes fears of letting go, scarcity, poor boundaries, and more. It's during the 0-7 years that we learn about where we fall in our relationships with siblings, parents, and our community and how we relate to them.

Physical manifestations can include joint pain, lower backache, elimination problems, obesity, constipation, anorexia, and poor immune system function.

Getting past or transcending unloving imprints involve cleansing, balancing, and healing for this root chakra.

The second chakra (orange/lower abdomen) houses our ability to accept others and develop new experiences. It's our sense of abundance, relationships, creativity, well-being, pleasure, sexuality, control, and money. This is where we are individuals; separate from our parents. It is here where we learn about the polarity of opposites, male and female, positive and negative. Relationships with the opposite sex are explored here.

Blocks here bring lessons on jealousy, betrayal, control, and power plays. Health issues can include uterine or bladder problems, sexual difficulties, impotence, lack of flexibility, sciatica, lower back pain, and problems with large intestines. I worked on a teenage girl once who had a block and what seemed like a shield of armor over this area. She had severe intestinal pains and her bowels were impacted. The doctors could not find anything physically wrong with her and gave her medication to counteract the symptoms.

It took us several sessions to clear this and get to the emotional root of the problem. I saw her as a fraternal twin in my meditation and I asked her if she had been a twin, thinking that the twin had died.

She had not been a twin.

I realized I had been given a message but that I had added my own interpretation of the imagery to it. I shared the imagery with her and asked her if that meant anything to her. She started to cry and told me she was transgender and she wanted to be a boy and she was deathly afraid of telling her parents.

That's an extreme example of course, but after we cleared the energy and removed the walls and balanced her, she stopped having intestinal pains and constipation and was off all medication within two weeks. She eventually told her parents – months later – and they are dealing with it the best they can.

Consider these questions to identify any issues:

1. Do you express your creativity?
2. Are you comfortable with your sexuality?
3. Can you receive nurturing from others?
4. Are you addicted to alcohol, drugs, sex, people or something else?

5. Do you suffer from guilt, shame, anger, and judgment towards the past?

6. Do you find it difficult to make money?

7. Do you stand up for yourself...say what you mean and mean what you say?

Transcending these imbalances means we need to feel, accept, love, and forgive emotional addictions.

The third chakra (golden yellow/above belly button, below chest) represents our self-confidence and control over our lives. It represents our ability to take action, our self-esteem, and expressing our personal power. A healthy third chakra is mastery of our emotions, self-confidence, intellect, and warmth. It also balances the two chakras before it. An unhealthy third chakra can result in fear of rejection, uncontrolled temper, blaming and demanding, fear of anything new, judgmental attitudes, aloofness, and low self-esteem. It is here we learn of self-empowerment, integrity, and self-respect. Consider how you feel when you make a huge mistake – or you feel ashamed. A lot of people experience "a stomachache".

Physical manifestations can result in diabetes, hypoglycemia, gallstones, nervousness, low energy, muscle cramps, stomach problems, lumbar spine, and liver disorders.

Consider these questions:

1. Do you compensate for low self-esteem and shame-based feelings by being overly responsible?

2. Are you afraid of change?

3. Can you follow your heart to break through blocks or fears?

4. Do you maintain your integrity by following through on what you say?

A good healing mantra here is: I balance my intuition and my intellect.

The fourth chakra, the heart chakra (chest center/teal green), represents our ability to love. It handles emotions like love, joy, and inner peace. It's also the integration point of the seven other chakras focused on here. It holds the sacred spark of the divine and the intuition of the Mother.

A healthy, open heart chakra allows us to forgive and have a healthy immune system and lungs. Think of the term "heavy heart". What does that actually mean? It means we are holding guilt, anger, and resentment – thereby "weighing" down the heart. I carried a heavy heart for a long time and I didn't even know it. When I meditated on it to clear it and balance it, it didn't work because I had not acknowledged my suppressed emotions and consequently, did not let them surface, heal, and go. There was no room in my heavy heart for healing because the negativity trapped there took up all the space. Once I acknowledged the trauma of the events in my life, once I *accepted the difficulty* of them, I was indeed able to transcend them.

Health issues that manifest here include high blood pressure, breathing difficulties, circulation problems, shortness of breath, chest pains, disorders of the heart, and tension between the shoulders. We also hold grief in our lungs, which is why news of grief often makes us feel like we can't breathe.

A good healing mantra here is: Healing my spirit, emotions, body, and heart take precedence over everything.

The fifth chakra (blue/throat) represents our self-expression and ability to communicate. It's important to note here that communication involves more listening than speaking. It represents choice, willpower, and the right to speak our truths. What we say, however, can empower or disempower us – depending on from where the thought is emanating. This is a powerful manifestation chakra for what we really want in life. A healthy throat chakra gives us clear, true voices. Remember that this chakra is the one between the head and the heart – so keeping this balanced creates synchronicity in those two areas. Remember when we talked about brain and heart energies? Creating synchronicity here is crucial and powerful.

Blocks in this area means our voices are weak and our ability to communicate what we want is clouded and confused. Physical manifestations include fever, ear infections, weariness, thyroid problems, disorders in the throat, ears, voice, neck, cervical spine, and hypothalamus and esophagus problems.

Ask yourself these questions:

1. Do you express your thoughts and feelings so others understand?

2. Is your voice clear and resonant when you speak?

3. Do you believe you have the right to make choices for yourself that empower you?

4. Are you a good listener?

5. Do you lie in order to get your way or smooth over a situation?

6. Do you have a good sense of timing and rhythm?

7. Are your head and your heart going in opposite directions?

A good mantra here is: I accept and embrace newfound awareness and direction.

The sixth chakra is the third eye chakra (indigo/between the eyebrows). This is our intuitive area as well as our ability to see and focus on the big picture. It's also imagination, wisdom, and decision-making.

It is known as the spiritual eye that seeks the truth in everything. A healthy third eye chakra allows us to perceive on multiple levels: not just what the actual eye sees, but the unspoken words, "reading between the lines", and inner knowledge. Remember when we talked about the energy in a room — when you know something is off? That's this chakra. Blocks in this area can cause delusions, indifference, poor memories, worry, and poor concentration.

To clear and balance this chakra, we need to trust our intuition and allow our imaginations to visualize beyond "the sky's the limit" mentality. I always think of J.B. S. Haldane's famous quote: "The universe is not only queerer than we suppose, but queerer than we *can* suppose."

We limit ourselves to thinking within our own little worlds, and in doing so, shut the door on our potential. Physical health issues for a blocked third eye chakra can result in headaches or migraines, eye problems, pituitary and pineal glands, and neurological problems.

A good balancing mantra here is: I balance the physical and the mental.

Our crown chakra, the seventh chakra (white/crown of the head) allows us to be connected completely to our source/God/Higher Power/Angels. It rules inner and outer beauty and feelings of bliss.

This chakra spins quickly and constantly when open. This chakra is our life force connection to our creator. It moves through all the chakras and connects them, so that we can be filled with God's grace and live in harmony.

Blocks in this chakra cause confusion, depression, senility, fear of success, and lack of inspiration. The flow of spiritual energy is blocked in both directions. This can create spiritual addiction and overintellectualizing, as well as dissociation with the body.

Physical health issues can be migraines, brain tumors, coma, amnesia, nervous system and muscular system disorders, mental issues, and skin disorders.

Think about your level of inspiration. Do you feel inspired? Open to new ideas? Do you feel depressed and powerless a lot of the time? Are you always complaining about your unhappiness?

A balancing mantra here is: my Father/God/etc. are one in complete harmony with my will and my greatest good.

It's interesting to connect the dots here with energy centers and physical ailments. Phrases such as "lump in my throat" and "heavy heart" really resonate with me for their respective chakras.

So here you have cleansing and balancing mantras and a start to bringing meditation and awareness into your life.

Interestingly enough, the word "meditate" derives from the Latin word for contemplate, from a base meaning 'to measure' as in mete out. Meditation is contemplation, which we all know how to do. I recommend bringing excitement and enthusiasm to beginning this practice. And since we're into the etymology portion of the program, the word "enthusiasm" comes from the Greek word *enthousiasmos*, which consists of the root words "theos" (God) and "en" (in) and "asm" breath. It literally means "breath of God" or "God within". The word "inspire" is from Middle English *enspire*, meaning to 'breathe or blow into.' The word was originally used of a divine or supernatural being, in the sense of 'imparting a truth or idea to someone.'

Just as with words, we have a very long history of existing and surviving without modern medicine. Obviously, or we would not be here. Understand that I am not negating modern medicine at all. Modern medicine and science have helped just about everyone I know at some point in their lives. I cannot imagine surgery without painkillers. I'm not a martyr. If I'm in physical pain, I want a painkiller. I personally celebrate all the scientists and doctors in this book that did the research I needed to find.

Meditation and chakra balancing are just components of a great way of life. They're great as a standalone treatment or in tandem with traditional medicines and treatments.

The difference is that if I am in emotional pain, I can now trace the root of it, identify it, release it, and begin to heal.

You can too.

But just as we practice, practice, practice the piano to get to Carnegie Hall, we need to practice, practice, practice happiness to reach our own potentials for balanced, joy-filled lives.

I leave you with the lyrics of one of my favorite songs by Snatam Kaur:
May the longtime sunshine upon you
All love surround you
May the pure light within you guide your way on.

Love and light,
Maureen

Reference materials and sources

1 OCTOBER 1, 2015 SCIENCE MAGAZINE

2 HTTPS://MINDUP.ORG/

3 mindful.org in August 2015./Makiko Kitamura Bloomberg November 21, 2013

4 http://www.mindbodygreen.com/0-2776/5-Facts-You-May-Not-Know-About-OM.html

5 Dr. Bradley Nelson/https://www.healerslibrary.com/heart-wall/

6 https://en.wikipedia.org/wiki/Magnetocardiography

7 http://www.sharedwisdom.com/page/soul-retrieval

8 http://www.2012-spiritual-growth-prophecies.com/chakra-symbols.html

Sources:

(1) Journal of Consciousness Exploration & Research | November 2013 | Vol. 4 | Issue 9 | pp. 977-987 Deshpande, P. B., Madappa, K. P., & Korotkov, K., Can the Excellence of the Internal Be Measured? – A Preliminary Study

(2) Jakovleva E, Korotkov K., Electrophotonic Analysis in Medicine. GDV Bioelectrography research. 2013. 160 p. Amazon.com.

(3) Pehek J. O., Kyler, H. J., and Foust, D.L., Image Modulation in Corona Discharge Photography, Science, Vol. 194, 263-270, October 1976.

(4) Source: http://powerthoughtsmeditationclub.com/the-chakras/

Source: http://www.collective-evolution.com/2014/03/15/scientists-quantify-graphically-chart-energy-of-human-chakras-in-various-emotional-states/